"Leading Big Brother Big Sister of Atlanta is walking the talk of leading by doing shaping, the next generation of leaders"

SCOTT UZZELL
PRESIDENT, CONVERSE

"Where would any of us be without the love, often tough love, and support of special people in our lives called mentors. Credibility is key in making the mentoring relationship work. Kwame, with the help of mentors, had the courage to change the direction and trajectory of his life. Now he has the courage to share that journey with others. Kwame has the credibility to make a significant difference for a young person facing similar difficult choices and who will one day be looking back over his or her life thinking, where would I be without the love and support of this special person in my life."

KATHY WALLER
RETRIED CFO, THE COCA-COLA COMPANY

"Kwame Johnson is a collaborative and authentic servant leader who has taught so many of us about faith and redemption. His life's work illuminates the importance and urgent priority of investing in our youth. Keep on lifting as you climb, Brother Kwame!!!"

ALBERT G. EDWARDS
PRESIDENT AND CEO- CERM
PRESIDENT- ATLANTA BUSINESS LEAGUE

"Shaping another's future for the better by empowering them to achieve is one of the most enjoyable and fulfilling things a person can do. We have the power to effect change and a shared responsibility to raise our voices, give our time, and open our heart to make a difference. We are blessed that Kwame Johnson, Sr. has chosen to graciously present his personal journey and unique leadership as proof positive that successful mentorship is our true legacy."

ERNEST L. GREER,
PRESIDENT, GREENBERG TRAURIG, LLP

"Kwame's story of resilience serves as an inspiration to all of us—youth and adults alike. His ability to build strong connections with others is the reason Kwame is an impactful leader, who knows first-hand the importance of mentorship and empowering young people. Kwame lives his truth everyday and as a leader in the Big Brothers Big Sisters network, he is a part of the village to ensure more youth will have the opportunity to have a mentor in their lives".

ARTIS STEVENS
PRESIDENT & CEO
BIG BROTHERS BIG SISTERS OF AMERICA

DEDICATION

I want to dedicate this book to the next generation of young leaders. I challenge you to always give back and do your part to make the world a better place.

DECLARATION

The term mentorship is uncommon in Latin. When you look at the foundation of Mentorship, the core is truly about relationships. Mentorship is likened to family in many other geographical regions outside of America. And thus, the defined term of mentorship is not needed because it is understood that you treat others as your family by leading them, guiding them, and caring for them. It is my firm belief that mentorship can change lives and defend the potential of people. I have witnessed many people realize their full potential through the power of mentorship. My goal is to be an integral part of the fabric for the tapestry of mentorship in America. My vision is to assemble an army of mentors above the limitations of race, religion, ethnicity or gender, or preference. Mentorship is something we all can do. And when we are all willing to reach back, we will realize a different world, with an abundance of humanity and goodness for all mankind.

ACKNOWLEDGEMENTS

- My parents, Oliver and Paulette Johnson, for always supporting me.
- Sabria and KJ, for keeping me whole.
- My brothers and sisters, for always having my back.
- My day one friends DJ, CJ, Dequan, Aaron, and Ricky.
- Mrs. Nunn, for all the love.
- Alan Rosenthal and Marsha Weissman, for defending my potential.
- Coach Maynard, for going to bat for "all of us."
- My home by the sea friends Vance and Jessie, who continue to support me
- Bob Woodson and Terence Mathis, for taking a chance on me.
- The BBBS board, staff, and donors, who have enabled me to serve.

THE
HOPE
INSIDE

CONTENTS

Introduction: The Foundation

No structure worth building can be constructed in the absence of a solid foundation.

|KJ|

Stories are powerful. Our stories allow us to see within ourselves and to extract the potential that lies inside due to the trials and successes that we have faced. I didn't truly recognize how powerful stories could be until I openly told my own story for the first time in a job interview. With palms sweaty and my nerves on edge, I discovered my power in moments of pure vulnerability in front of what would be my future employer. Because I had shared my story, I was hired into my first leadership role, and it has only gone up from there.

I am who I am because of my story and the everyday heroes who guided me along the way. Before I became the successful CEO that I am today, as a child, I was mentored by my family and my elderly neighbors, two sisters who gave me knowledge in exchange for snow shoveling and dusting. I watched people from my neighborhood die around me, losing themselves to the streets as I grew up. I fought relentlessly to stay neutral, balancing on a line of separation. This line represented two worlds. The world that I knew: the one with grocery store jobs, track practice, and friends that were still alive. And then there was the world that was beginning to surround and suffocate me. Until one day, I was pulled from that line and forced to choose a side, changing the course of my life for good.

During my Junior year of high school, I was fully involved in street life, hanging out, drugs, and eventually robbery. I was still working and attending school, but my life had spiraled away from me until I lost everything. My scholarship to University, school life, job, and freedom were all lost because I was a kid making the wrong decisions due to my circumstances. I ended up in prison, and despite all the painful nights, the loneliness, and through the ongoing work I put in and the mentoring I received along the way, I came out on top of it all.

From entering college to working down the street from the White House in my early twenties, I've lived a life many can't quite believe. When they look at me, they don't see the kid that I was, but through my line of work, I see that kid in the eyes of the children that I mentor. I see the scared kid that I was, and I see the potential. The potential that I, now a successful Black CEO and happy family man, have found within myself over the years through hard work, dedication, and with a little help from my community of friends and family.

For the first time ever, I will publicly share the series of events that shaped my life and my career. This story ultimately represents triumph in its purest form. Until writing this book, I had no idea of this story's power. Today, I know that it is the solid foundation from which my life was constructed. I am my story, and now this is my legacy I share with you.

Arthur Blank

Coach Maynord

Mom and Dad

Featured on Channel 46

Immediate Family

Dad with Mutumbo

1: ADAPTATION

*It is my belief that the words faith
and foundation are synonymous.*

|KJ|

A mentor once told me that, "To build a tall building, you must have a strong foundation." The building blocks of my life were established in Syracuse, New York, on the east side near Syracuse University. Born as the son of an undeniably strong woman, my mother was well known for her exercise of leadership and activism. She juggled multiple roles as a nurse, public servant, and school board member. She was recognized as the first African American woman to be elected as the board President for the Syracuse City Schools Board of Education. Although I did not realize it at the time, I attained a great deal of experience while accompanying her to the meetings on a regular basis. I learned how school systems ran, and the challenges boards in the region faced. My mom's ambitions inspired her to run for the city council. She didn't win; however, she demonstrated resilience amidst the race.

It was no secret that my parents wanted to make Syracuse a better place to live. They were just as persistent in their quest for excellence inside the home as they were outside of it. And that persistence meant that excellence was demanded of my four siblings and me. There was never a dull moment with two brothers and two sisters in the home, a set of dogs, and me. As the middle child, I would eventually establish my own perspective on family dynamics and my perception of the community. Our home, which my parents paid about $12,000 for, was situated just in front of Cherry Hill, a public housing complex. There seemed to always be something wrong with the house. From the plumbing to the roof, repairs were needed on a regular basis. My father was very frugal and used heating and air sparingly. In the north, the cold nights and drafts from the windows made their presence known. This is likely the reason why I keep the heat high in my home today.

The neighborhood resembled every other lower middle class city area when we first arrived. However, over time the exit of companies like General Motors, Chrysler, and Carrier contributed to slow deterioration. In addition, the neighborhood experienced a series of transitions as a result of drugs and springs of violence that began to plague the community. Today, Syracuse has one of the highest poverty rates in the country.

My father, who was from New York City, attended college on a track scholarship. He later earned his Master's degree from Syracuse University Maxwell School of Citizenship and Public Affairs after relocating in pursuit of a better life for his family. Being a sibling to thirteen brothers and sisters, he watched many of his siblings become hooked on drugs or dragged into the prison system. By watching this, he became persistent in his mission to prevent young people from falling victim to the circumstances around them. Only two of his siblings attended college, and he was one of them. Since drug abuse was so rampant in New York, where he had been raised, he made the decision to pursue a career as a health teacher. I can remember him hosting a series of *Say No to Drugs campaigns* to educate kids about the dangers of drugs. He used to set up booths at local grocery stores. Against our better judgment, my sister and I dressed up as clowns. Our assignment was to entice kids to come over to our table. Quite frankly, the execution left a lot to be desired, but his heart was in the right place.

In spite of everything around us, my father fought to ground my siblings and me in service, which also meant that he led with a stern hand. He was hard on us, and at times I questioned his approach. Today, I recognize that his actions were not without cause. He never wanted us to become products of our environment. He taught me the essence of grit and constantly reminded me that giving up was not an option. He would say, "You put the effort in. You work hard, and you train hard." He taught us that in life, excuses have no merit. We were responsible for shoveling the snow outside and walking to school, even in less than stellar temperatures. Strength was his love language. I can't recall when he spoke the words, "I love you," or anything of the sort. I wish he had spoken words that affirmed me emotionally, but in spite of it all, his presence in my life could never be questioned. He made his presence felt in so many other ways. He had this way of giving advice that crept into your soul. His words are still with me today.

On the weekends, I spent a great deal of time cleaning the house. Since there were so many inhabitants, the level of organization was never quite to my standard. Maybe it was my way of bringing order to my life, or perhaps I was a little obsessive about cleanliness. The house being clean made me calm. When it wasn't clean, I felt uneasy. My brothers and sisters did other tasks, but I was the keeper of order. We didn't have a washer or dryer, which meant that I often accompanied my parents to the laundromat. There were times when I'd have five bags of clothes, one for each of us at the house. Most kids my age would have had a problem with chores of this magnitude, but my focus was on having a clean house and clean clothes. On the days when I couldn't get a ride from my parents to the laundromat, I would put two bags on one handlebar and two on the other and ride my bike to the laundromat, wash the clothes and ride back home. The other cleaner and organizer in the house was my mom. She always moved around the house and cleaned up as best she could after so many people. This attribute likely came from her. Cleaning the way I did, taught me to be intentional and thorough, a skill set I would eventually apply in other areas of my life. I also recognized that there was power in teamwork at an early age. My parents were quite busy with work and giving their all to the community, so I pitched in where I could.

Another special attribute about our house was that it had a playroom. There were a multitude of toys passed down from my older brother and sister that filled the room. All the kids from the projects just behind our home would come to our house to play. We would often set up shop in the playroom, and on other occasions, we would find our way to the attic. There was an old mattress in the attic, and we would play karate. My father was a 7-degree black belt in Aikido. He had a Dojo which he required us to do in the early years. He taught at school on weekdays and afterward headed to the Aikido Dojo. When I was younger in elementary school, we were required to go to the dojo after school. I didn't really like it that much. It just wasn't my thing. By the time I entered middle school, he had recognized that I didn't love it and eventually no longer required us to participate, but he continued to hold practices. He also started a local track team in Syracuse outside of school sports. He acquired a small yellow school bus to transport students, and those who rode on the bus got made fun of for riding. To this day, I still don't know how he got it, but he used it to bring the kids from my neighborhood to different track meets all around the state of New York as we competed. My father's grit and determination are among two of the most coveted attributes I would like to believe I acquired. Coupled with my mother's personification of leadership and commitment, my parents were without question the building blocks of my foundation.

Cold Hands and Warm Hearts

Most kids my age were finding ways to be inside amidst the cold mornings in Syracuse. I, on the other hand, was in search of ways to make money. At the age of twelve, I started my first job as a snow shoveler. Syracuse is known for having the most snow in the country, so I had my work cut out for me. My first employers were my neighbors Ms. Nunn and Ms. Brown. They were sisters from the deep south who were well into their eighties and nineties. Ms. Brown grew up in Missouri cleaning white folks' houses. Ms. Nunn moved to New York with her husband, a worker on the railroads. He passed before I ever had the chance to meet him.

Back then, Ms. Nunn and Ms. Brown lived down the street from me on just $1,200 a month. I remember it like it was yesterday. Ms. Nunn was the old lady who sat on the porch and called the cops if you were running in the streets. Before I knew better, I thought she was mean. She was heavy-set with big ankles, a big stomach, lots of missing teeth, gray hair and glasses, and boy was she stern. Ms. Brown, her older sister, was the opposite. Slim and statuesque with grey hair, she was mildly toned and often very quiet. Ms. Nunn was loud and extroverted. And although I interacted with Ms. Brown often, I engaged with Ms. Nunn more. Ms. Brown stayed upstairs most of the time.

I met them both during a massive blizzard. In just a few days, we had acquired around five feet of snow. Everything in the city was shut down. Peering from the window and observing the elements, I had the bright idea to start a snow shoveling business. I decided at that moment that I would shovel snow for ten bucks. And on that same day, I walked directly to their house, and the snow was, as she described it, *above my head*. The rest was history. I was officially employed. Over the years, Ms. Nunn would describe the story of our meeting to everyone in the same way. She'd say, "I looked over the mountain of snow, and I could barely see his head. All I could hear was a little voice saying, 'Hey, do you need someone to shovel your snow?'"

On the first day I shoveled, she kept coming out and checking on me. She was worried that the job was too much for me to handle. Two hours later, I came in to collect the ten dollars I'd earned.

She said to me, "It'd be nice to have you help around the house. I'd love to have you come back on another day."

From that day forward, I was officially booked and busy. She invited me to start cleaning her house and shopping for her groceries. I learned a great deal about furniture, including what a settee and a brazier were in the process. Not long after I showed myself approved with the errands, she taught me to cook. Each time I went to her home, we prepared meals together. She taught me how to make breakfast and her recipes for tea cakes and eggs. She paid me by the hour, but we both lost track of time. The helping hands and the company trumped the wages. She shared stories about her life and the different life lessons she acquired along the way. And because I had never met my grandparents on either side, Ms. Nunn became the grandmother I never had.

My mom was from Cleveland, Ohio, and met my father in college. She came from a well-off family. Her father, Paul White, was a legend in Cleveland. He was the first Black partner at BakerHostetler, a local and international law firm. He was also the first Black elected judge in the state of Ohio. When my mother met my father, her parents disapproved of him, and they disowned her for deciding to start a family with him because he grew in poverty in the mean streets of New York. Paul White, my grandfather, died when I was in high school. I never shook his hand or made his acquaintance. That's how deep the hatred ran. Growing up, I was not aware of the full scope of the story. I didn't know why we never visited our grandparents on my mother's side. Our grandparents on my father's side died before I was born, but I was well aware of the fact that my mom's father and mother were alive. Yet, we never spoke of them in our home. And I never inquired about it because my mother didn't bring it up, so I didn't bring it up. Although she came from a wealthy family in Cleveland, Ohio, she was a struggling nurse trying to make ends meet alongside her husband. And because everyone in my home was busy with real life, I will forever be grateful to Ms. Nunn and Ms. Brown for filling the holes in my soul that I didn't realize were empty at the time.

$2 SPECIAL

Walking to school in Syracuse was a great feat. There was plenty of snow to trek through. The crew consisted of Charles, Ricky, Chutney, Mark, and of course me. Luckily, our trek was less than a mile. The older I got, the more my love for music grew. I'd carry a huge Sony boom box on my shoulders and play music as we walked. The big Double D batteries gave it enough juice to play the mixtapes I acquired with all the latest jams. We listened to everything from DJ Clue to DJ Juice. This was the early 90's so the music coming from New York was a vibe. By the time we arrived at school, breakfast was being served. And because we had free breakfast and lunch for everybody, eating was not optional. Just before breakfast, we'd make a pit stop to the gym to play basketball. In the gym, I was able to play my music even louder than when we walked the streets of the neighborhood. My radio was so powerful the sound could be heard from outside. So we'd go from the gym, everybody socializing and playing basketball, to breakfast and then to our respective classes. Some teachers were more impactful than others. Miss Kent, my math teacher, believed in us. Her first words were, "You're gonna start this class with an A. It's up to you to keep that A."

Her words spoke volumes about her approach to education and how she perceived what we could achieve. She encouraged us to sit in front of the class, and we actually performed well. She was a phenomenal teacher.

After school each day, we walked to a local store to hang out. Back then, we thought it was cool to smoke cigarettes just outside the store. From the store, we walked to the park to play basketball once more. At the time, I aspired to be an NBA star. On most days, we had to shovel snow just to see the actual court. And on some Fridays, when I didn't hang out with the guys, I joined my father at the Masjid. He converted to Islam when I was in middle school. Outside of school, I spent little time at home. Both my mom and dad were always working or busy, so I knew that I could use the time as I saw fit. There weren't a lot of quality interactions taking place once we were all older. My older siblings were off to college by the time I reached middle school. There were three of us left in the house. We did not gather around the table for dinner together.

On many days my dinner was my responsibility. Some days, I'd swing by my house, drop my book bag off and leave back out on foot. I'd walk down through the projects and past the corner store. That pathway revealed a great deal of turmoil. Visions of guys hanging out smoking and drinking were ingrained in my mind. We would all say, "what's up" but I knew better than to stop. I'd walk until I reached Burger King. I ate there pretty much every day, especially after they launched the $2 special. With the special, I'd get two burgers and two fries. It was a deal that could not be beaten. Going to Burger King was me fending for myself. Doing so also freed me from being trapped in the house. Even when I was not out with my friends at the park, I never wanted to sit in the house and play video games. That was never me. I was always outside. And because my parents gave me that flexibility which I think was good, the community became my domain. The more time that I spent in the community, the more I assumed ownership of the remnants of turmoil associated with it. As I got older, not all of my friends continued pursuing their education, but they were still my friends. I was now in the company of people with whom I no longer shared core values. Our commonality was directly rooted in the agreement surrounding the use of our idle time.

"THE FIRST FRIEND I LOST."

By the time I reached eighth grade, the community that I had looked to for love evolved into mean streets that consumed life. For the first time in my life, I came face to face with death. I watched as an onlooker as the streets began to swallow folks whole. The loss of life and hope for a better tomorrow took a toll on everyone. I noticed a trend of kids I'd known from elementary school dropping out of middle school during the seventh grade. Charles, Ricky, Chutney, and Mark began to forge their own paths in the community.

After I noticed the trend of friends dropping out of school, I started to associate more with friends that were from different communities. In middle school, all kinds of people would come together for the first time from other regions, which meant access to more people. I began making new friends and engaging in more formalized team sports, which became a part of my daily itinerary. As I hit puberty, my interest in girls was also activated. And because the girls were in school, that was where I wanted to be despite what everyone else was doing. The stories on the news about people getting killed all the time in Syracuse were growing in number. Every month someone's death was reported. Reports about people being killed within blocks of where I lived started to become normal. Then the dreadful day when someone you know is reported changes you forever. At some point in our eighth-grade year, Mark replaced school for acts of armed robbery. He garnered a reputation on the streets as a stick-up kid. One day, Mark robbed the wrong person. The guy came to his house and shot him with a shotgun loaded with pellets. He lost his life that day. It was right down the street from my house. It was hurtful for sure when it happened to Mark. The unfortunate factor about growing up amidst turmoil is that you expect moments of loss. You anticipate them. It is tragic to think that there are communities of people just waiting for loss. After Mark died, we kept going. The black hole that swallowed humans whole closed back up until fate and circumstance summoned, reopening the pit to consume the next victim. In retrospect, my parents should have moved away from the community when my older brother and sister went to college, but they stayed trying to change the community. Instead, the community would eventually change us.

Brothers United Participants

Bob Woodson and Terence Mathis

Interviewing Bernie Sanders

King Middle School

2: ALTERATION

Transition precedes transformation.

|KJ|

OLD SOUL POP

The transition between middle and high school taught me to be strategic and, more importantly, cautious. My character didn't change during this transition, only my surroundings and my response to them. I was still the same kid hanging out with Ms. Nunn and Ms. Brown when my schedule permitted. And even though I was still just a kid, I was always an old soul.

Throughout the neighborhood and even my family knew me as old soul Pop. It was a nickname given to me by my mom when I was around two years old. She explained that I always acted older than I was. By the age of three, I spoke fluently. Even today, people think I'm older than I actually am. I have always been curious, which led to my inquisitiveness. Add in a hint of mischievousness that soon surfaced and ushered me into a few compromising scenarios.

The acquisition of new friends from new communities meant new situations to navigate. For some, it was a time to become introduced and acclimated to gang life. For others, it triggered the onset of tumultuous rivalries. None of those things interested me.

I was more of a person that would say, "Let's go play basketball, talk to the girls, or let's go hang out."

I learned how to maintain my identity while not getting caught up in all the riff raff that zoning districts established to make us feel that we were more different than alike. The key was to never fully associate with a particular block. No one could say they heard me proclaiming where I was from. Although it was no secret that I grew up on the east side, I learned not to limit my relationships to a particular geographical location. After witnessing the limitations, enemies garnered, and misplaced frustration that other guys experienced who claimed one block or another, I knew better than to travel down that road. My quest to expand the scope of my relationships and alliances manifested in connecting with a few groups of older guys. Eventually, I learned that I was ill-prepared for much of what would come my way.

GRAPPLING WITH THE TRUTH

Most kids welcome their first day of high school without much excitement. Not me. On my first day of high school, I witnessed a brawl in the hallway. Things got so out of hand that the fight spilled over into a special ed classroom. There were multiple participants, and chairs were flying from every direction. A teacher even got knocked out in the scuffle. Some older guys from the eastside got into it with some guys from the southside.

As a bystander, I could only deduce that high school would be much different from middle school. Right then and there, I accepted the fact that the days of innocently walking in the snow and enduring the elements with my big boom box propped atop my shoulder just to make it to breakfast at school were gone. There had been a couple of fights here and there in middle school, but never a massive brawl like what I witnessed that day. And while I was well aware that there would potentially be conflicts, I never had to deal with any of this magnitude in middle school. This was my first time being exposed to that kind of neighborhood clash in the four walls of my high school building.

During this transition period, I spent less and less time with Ms. Brown and Ms. Nunn. Their love was something that never left my spirit or memory. As time passed, I sought employment in another capacity. After interviewing, I landed a new role as a stock boy at Wegmans Grocery Store. I worked whenever possible. My routine included taking the bus to Wegman's after school and on the weekends. It was about seven miles from our house. As a gainfully employed young man, making my own money, I set my sights on obtaining my driver's license by my sixteenth birthday. I trekked through two feet of snow to take the test on that day, and I passed with flying colors. My tenth-grade year was spent attending school, working, and hanging out. My dreams of playing in the NBA were ever-present. And although I was good enough to play on a team in middle school, the competition once in high school increased. There was more talent, and the stakes were higher. Unfortunately, the skillset or talent to thrive at the Varsity level weren't there for me.

At the time, if you were not a starter or a prospect for the varsity team, then you knew that there was not a future in sports for you. My hoop dreams faded by the middle of my sophomore year, and I redirected my athletic ability towards track and field. My family had a natural ability for running track, which meant that excelling in the sport was in my DNA. My sister ran track in college, as well as my brother. My father placed second in the NY State Championship for the 100M Dash and then attended college on a full scholarship. Running was a natural ability in our bloodline. There are times when life makes tough decisions about who and what we should be when we don't have the strength to do so for ourselves. This era was one of those moments for me.

CHOICES

To my surprise, track became a sport that I looked forward to competing in. Discovering another way to ignite my athletic ability led me to love the sport. The more I ran, the more I found my groove on the track and in my personal life.

I met Lala—my first love—while at school. Lala lived with her mom in an apartment at Springfield Gardens, a public housing complex. My parents didn't like that she grew up there. I don't think they disliked her; more so, they disliked her environment and her family dynamic. The notion of me hanging out at her house while her mother was dating a known drug dealer wasn't a recipe for success. My parents believed that dating her would hinder my growth.

Lala's mom was a lovely lady. She welcomed me into her home. We were allowed to go into Lala's room and close the door. That would have never happened at my house. I could never bring a girl into my room in my house. Girls could come into my house, but I could never bring one in my room, let alone close the door. Lala's mom was much less reserved. And because of her flexibility, I spent a great deal of time at their home. It became my favorite place to hangout, and even where I ate dinner on many nights. I never spent the night, but I would stay until late.

By the time I reached eleventh grade, my schedule was a mixture of school, track, Lala, and the streets.

Somewhere between track meets and my budding relationship, I became intrigued by the allure of the streets. There was a mystique behind the money to be made amidst a fast lifestyle. I made some money, but I wanted more. Perhaps I wanted to be more self-sufficient while doing more for Lala. Maybe I wanted to be more respected in the streets. Whatever the underlying cause was, I was certain that the streets began calling my name in a way it never had before.

The summer before my junior year, my family planned a trip to New York City to get more clothing for school. We always traveled to the city to do our school shopping because my father's family still lived there. The trip provided us with an opportunity to visit all of our aunts, uncles, cousins, extended family, and friends from Mount Vernon and the Bronx. On this particular trip, Lala was scheduled to come with me, but she eventually considered backing out since she did not have any money to attend. This was a pivotal moment and point for me because I assumed the role of a provider. I owned the responsibility of figuring out how I could get extra money to help Lala and her family out financially.

Maintaining my job at Wegmans and continually increasing my hours was a means to boost my earning potential. I was doing well financially for a kid in his junior year of high school while sharing a portion of my earnings with Lala and her mother. However, the acquisition of the provider role would lead me down a rabbit hole, forcing me to seek new ways to make more money at all costs.

I'll admit, the newly discovered ambition wasn't all for Lala and her mother. I, too, wanted more things, one of them being my own car. Eventually, I got one. That was a big deal for me. I bought a grey Mazda 626, for approximately $7,000 with a loan through my father's credit union. My parents allowed me to finance it, yet again demonstrating their trust for me. I was one of the only kids driving to school in their own car at sixteen. Once the car was mine, my next move was to add some sound. One measure of how cool you were was the sound that came from your car. The goal was to have the loudest sound system. Unlike the south, where loud music means lots of bass, it's all about high, loud vocals in the north. You could hear me three blocks away playing Mary J Blidge over a Biggie Smalls beat. Lala and I would ride around like a modern-day Bonnie and Clyde. At times, I felt invincible behind the wheel. I earned everything I had. No one gave me anything. I was proud of what I made happen for myself and for Lala. Having the car also meant I had a new surge of power. I was exposed to a new world because I now had access to all of Syracuse whenever I wanted. I could drive to the mall or even the southside at any given moment. I started driving through different blocks just out of curiosity. I observed guys who live on the southside that people from where I lived didn't get along with. There were around seven different blocks on the south side. In addition to the mall, I would also venture to the park to meet up with different groups of people.

More access also meant more girls and more experiences. At some point, my friends and I had fake IDs made. We immediately began putting them to use at local nightclubs. Club Mirage was up first. The ID worked, and once inside, my first stop was the bar. I had never consumed alcohol before, so I had no idea what to order. I decided I would just copy what somebody else ordered. That, someone, was a young lady who ordered a Sex On The Beach. I had no idea it wasn't considered to be a *man's drink* per se, so I ordered one right after she did. For a couple of years thereafter, Sex On The Beach was my drink of choice.

By the time I reached eleventh grade, I was living a double life. Friends, the club, and girls became the priorities. Meanwhile, school, work, and track, all areas in which I excelled, appealed less to me. Driving around town, buying clothes, and going to the clubs on the weekends held my attention, as they were events to which I looked forward. Oddly enough, I was still spending time with Ms. Nunn and Ms. Brown, but my priorities were shifting. By the summer of tenth grade transitioning into the eleveth grade, transitioning into the twelfth grade, I was forced to pick a side.

Thornden Park was a block from my house and was the spot on the weekends. On Sundays, more people were drawn to the location because of the car show. Both sides of the streets would be lined up with cars and onlookers. It would take an hour and a half just to drive through the park. There was always music playing and barbecues in motion. Traditionally, we played three-on-three basketball tournaments during the summer months. In particular, one day, a team from the south side came to play. They arrived on a big school bus. That day, it seemed like the whole eastside was there. There had to have been at least sixty guys. These were all my friends, and I was standing there with them. They decided to heckle and intimidate the southside team. Finally, the southside team made the decision to leave. Everyone there recognized the potential catastrophe that was at hand. When they got back on their bus, guys from the east side started throwing rocks at it. Some guys started jumping the kids from the southside, and others were trying to tip the bus over. The whole time I was just standing there, not doing anything, because I didn't have any real problems with any of the guys from the south side. Even so, the southside guys were looking out the windows of the bus, pointing at different people, and making threats of retaliation. After that day, I suspected that aligning with a side would soon be my only option.

THE ONLY WAY OUT IS THROUGH

A few weeks after the incident at the park, I was almost jumped while leaving the mall with one of my friends. We were going to catch the last bus home, or at least that's what we thought. Thirty guys, many faces I recognized from the southside, approached us. Luckily that day, we managed to get away, but I was now well aware of the fact that regardless of whether I chose a side or not, one had been selected for me.

Two weeks later, while at work, I learned one of the guys on the southside bus that day also worked at Wegmans. He was a pretty big-time guy known to have killed people before– and is currently in prison for killing people. Tony worked in the meat department on most days, but on this day, he showed up in response to my call for assistance while bagging groceries for a customer.

He walked right up to me and said, "We gonna get you."

That's when it hit me. Tony was a real guy, not some random person I heard stories about. It was even more unsettling because I didn't even know he worked there. After the work incident and almost getting jumped at the mall, I knew I had to choose a side. I could no longer be a kid just going to school and running track. I tried my best to walk that fine line, but it no longer worked. The choice to remain neutral no longer existed. That's when I decided to go all in. I started claiming Lex, a neighborhood on the east side behind my house. I fully associated myself with those guys. If I went to the mall, I would no

28

longer go by myself. I went with at least ten guys. If they were going to go to the movies or the club, I would go with them. Before, I had no problem frequenting those places by myself or even with a girl. They traveled with at least ten to twenty people at all times because they always had beef outside of the eastside. I now needed them to be safe.

The association made it easier for me to move around. Once you're seen or associated with a group, you also assume ownership of all the conflicts and problems that they have. Luckily, I was never with them when tragedy struck. The byproduct of my alliance and now allegiance was poor decision-making. Fully immersed in the group, I met Jorge, a Spanish guy. He was a member of the east side but very much a leader in his own right. He moved a little differently and a little more independently, which was in alignment with who I already was. General mischief evolved into selling drugs and robbing drug dealers.

In my mind, all of the activities that we prioritized made sense. It was easier to make a big score rather than hanging out at the corner selling dimes all day long. We devised a strategy around hitting up drug houses, and I was down. All the while, I was still going to school, working at Wegmans, running track, and dropping by to check on Ms. Nunn and Ms. Brown periodically. The unfiltered truth is that I was living two lives at the time and willing to risk them both for the sake of money.

Kwame Mentee Little
Brother Anthony

First Ladies Laura Bush
and Jill Biden

ATL Mayor Andrew Dickens

John Collins

My Parents, Brothers, Sisters

Governor Brian Kemp

3: UNFOLD

*When we believe ourselves to be imprisoned,
we fail to recognize our possession
of the keys to set ourselves free.*

|KJ|

With money as the root of my ambition, I no longer saw the world as I once had. In my mind at the time, the need, want and desire to acquire more money and more clout in the streets was equivalent to accessing more freedom. Of all the things I've ever desired in life, freedom is the objective I wanted most. This mindset justified my actions and a rightful means to an end. Jorge had gotten some information about some guys who were moving weight on a higher level. They traveled to Syracuse from New York City to do a deal.

We heard they were staying in a hotel, and our goal was to find them and take ownership of whatever they had.

Jorge was in possession of an AK47 for protection due to some previous issues on the streets that left him shot and robbed. He was no longer willing to leave himself in harm's way. The AK47 was all the protection he needed, and he was ready, willing, and able to protect his life and his possessions. Having an AK47 was unheard of at the time in Syracuse. Most people didn't have access to that kind of weaponry for a myriad of reasons. Jorge's possession of a weapon of that magnitude spoke to both his level of connection and his mindset. With the AK47 in tow, we made our way to the hotel.

When we arrived, they weren't there. It was bad information and bad news for us. Back then, I was furious. This was going to be a big robbery and score us a huge financial win. Once we realized the information was bad, Jorge and I decided to leave and cut our losses. Just as we began walking back towards the car, a clerk at the front desk saw us, AK47 in hand, and yelled, "We're gonna call the cops!" There was an element of panic for both Jorge and me as it was not something we planned for, but the one thing we had in common was getting the money by any means necessary. Since we weren't successful in taking it from the guys in their hotel room, we made a split-second decision to get the money from the hotel front desk. The stakes were now much higher, and the blueprint for our success shifted. We were no longer robbing drug dealers. We were now committing armed robbery against a business with the possibility of a casualty of war. It was dumb and the wrong thing to do. Today, I recognize without question that there are no excuses to justify our behavior. We were caught up in the moment and not in a position to make sound decisions.

After we managed to get the money from the front desk without harming anyone, we exited as fast as possible, hopped in the car, and sped off. Although we were driving quickly, we did not believe that it was enough to bring up any suspicions, but in the end, it would not matter. Just as we drove away from the hotel, the glare of blue and red lights forced its way into our car from behind. At that moment, I felt like my heart sank to my feet. My breathing was rapid, and my hands shook as Jorge pulled the car over. We could hear the officer's footsteps echoing off the pavement as he approached the driver's side of the vehicle.

Once Jorge lowered the window, the cop leaned in and stared into the car with a steady gaze before stating, "There's been a robbery at a hotel down the street. We're looking for the individuals who match the description we've been given."

To our surprise, we actually didn't fit the description. Somebody must have gotten something wrong in the haste of giving the information to the cops. We lied and said that we were just out visiting some friends and heading home. The officer was preparing to let us go and told us that he would run our licenses as a standard procedure—that's when the situation deteriorated. My license checked out fine, but Jorge's license was flagged. He happened to be out of prison on parole and out past his curfew. Unbeknownst to me, Jorge had priors. And because of his past, that gave the police the legal right to search the vehicle. There was nothing we could do at the moment. They found everything, the money, the gun, and the suspects they had been searching for. Jorge and I were transported to jail around eleven o'clock that night.

The police began interrogating us about the robbery in the car. And because I knew nothing about the criminal justice system, I didn't even ask for a lawyer. I was completely unaware of the steps I needed to take to protect myself and my legal rights. This single moment still ignites my fire to educate young people on the criminal justice system and their rights. This is not to say that young people should break the law, but they should at least understand their rights.

ONE CALL CAN CHANGE EVERYTHING

At around two in the morning, after a long stint of interrogation, one of the officers said, "We've got to call your parents." I was unaware that there was yet another level of anxiety possible that I could experience. I remember thinking, *how do I call my mom and tell her I'm downtown? How am I going to explain this to her?* I was speechless and unwilling to make the call, so I didn't. The police did. I think they might have put me on the phone, but I can't remember because I had mentally checked out. Afterward, they transported us downtown and put us into the general population. Later, I would learn that the robbery and the gun were classified as violent offenses. I was now facing conviction for five felonies, and my bail was set around $50,000. It started to sink in for me just how big of a deal this was. All I could do was wonder what would happen and what the sentence for a crime of this magnitude could be.

About two days later, my lawyer Allen Rosenthal, a family friend my parents hired to defend me, came down to the jail. He had gone to college with my parents, and they were young adults growing up in Syracuse together after college. My parents called him to see what he could do to help. He didn't say much. I asked him if he could get me out? He looked at me with skepticism in his eyes and responded that he would work on it. I found out later, he wanted me to stay in there a few days just to let the experience sink in. I'm not sure if he was convinced that I was remorseful, but I was. News of the robbery spread like wildfire. From the front page of the local newspaper to national news outlets, the story was reported more than I could track. "17-YEAR-OLD CAUGHT WITH AK47 DURING A ROBBERY." It became a massive story that impacted the community adversely. The impact of my actions started to spill out onto my family. My mom, who served, felt the brunt of the headlines. One article read, "PAULETTE JOHNSON'S SON CAUGHT WITH AK47." Another article that was put out read: "SCHOOL BOARD MEMBER'S SON CAUGHT WITH AK47." I felt awful. People were going after my family for something I did, something I couldn't take back. My mom and dad had worked all those years to better the community, yet I was an accomplice in tearing it back down. Their reputations were now on the line. They continued to put everything on the line for me in true heroic fashion. They paid my bail, putting up our house as collateral. Because of them, I got to go home for a while. I didn't have to spend my time waiting for court while locked away in jail. It was a Saturday when I got out. That night, I had no desire to go to the club or hang out with the crew. The taste for a Sex On the Beach had miraculously disappeared. The nightlife, the girls, and even the block were not so glamorous anymore.

When Monday arrived, I attempted to go to school. I was stopped by the administration officer, who informed me that I had been kicked out for the rest of the year or until everything was resolved. I was innocent but guilty. It was not a secret or question of whether or not I had done the crime, but I had not gone to trial or been proven guilty of anything. Even so, I was well aware of the fact that everyone had given up on me. Wegmans was no different. I was notified that I was no longer employed at the store. They even pulled the scholarship they were going to give me for college. Innocent until proven guilty, right?

I was arrested on February 13th, in the winter season. My attorney eventually got it worked out where I would attend the trial through the winter, and the case would be finalized the day after I finished my junior year. Therefore, if I had been sentenced to any time, I would at least have completed my junior year of high school. With this plan in motion, I enrolled in night school while awaiting my fate in the court system. Everything between the arrest and the actual court date is a blur. When your life flashes before your eyes and the prospect of your freedom is in question, nothing else really matters.

The first time I went to court, I did not own a suit but heard how I needed to appear from the attorney. What I had at the time was a pair of black slacks, a white shirt, and somehow a pair of tuxedo shoes. It didn't really go together, but it's what I had. Upon entering the court, the judge—Judge Anthony Aloi— said, "Hey, you look pretty sharp with those tuxedo shoes." That day was the first time I heard all of my charges formally read.

On a few occasions, I heard the lawyers working on my case say, "Hey, we're going to need all hands-on deck."

Their goal was to get me sentenced as a youthful offender, also known as "YO." In New York at that time, gun laws were very tough. One year per bullet and five years for the gun. That was big in the '90s and the 2000s. Jorge's gun had approximately thirty bullets. The

numbers of what I was potentially facing speak for themselves. Getting charged as a minor versus being charged
as an adult was largely impactful. It could have been the
difference of reducing a sentence to the maximum of
five years to five years of probation. Not only would my
sentence be reduced as a youthful first-time offender,
but my record would also be sealed under the youthful
offender statute. That sounded better than the twenty or
thirty years we faced because of the gun and the bullets.

DIFFERENT SHIPS, SAME BOAT

My lawyer decided that we needed to get some community leaders together to advocate for me. He also got
me connected with an organization called the Center
for Community Alternatives (CCA). They had offices in
Syracuse and Brooklyn, and their primary mission was
to advocate for alternatives to incarceration. My lawyer,
along with Marsha Weissman, the founder, and CEO of
CCA, came together and curated a plan for the youthful
offender classification. We needed to get letters from my
school and local pastors. My parents and my track coach
Steve Manord also played a huge role in supporting me
during this time. They presented all of the information
to the judge and established a case. Our premises were
established on the following facts: I had never been in
trouble; I maintained a job; had a track scholarship, as

well as other opportunities for a promising pathway. They requested that I receive five years' probation. On the second court date, the judge agreed to the Youthful Offender classification based on that plan. That was a significant relief for my family. The possibility of five years in jail was still looming, but at least we overcame one hurdle. The Youthful Offender designation also sealed my record, so even if I had to serve five years in jail, my records would not be made public. I would never have to speak of the case again if I didn't want to.

The end of the school year earmarked my final court date— which was also my sentencing date. We worked closely with the district attorney's office on a probation strategy. When I went to the DA's office—who was the prosecutor in my case— the DA said, "We'll recommend probation to the judge if you can pass a lie detector test." This was the first time this option was presented, and I thought it was interesting.

He said, "We want to make sure this is the only thing you've ever done because if you did things in the past, we're not gonna offer probation." I knew that I had been hanging in the streets and doing other things, but the only way to get probation was to pass this lie detector test. I didn't tell my lawyer or my parents anything about the other stuff I had done. I agreed to take the test and my chances.

In my opinion, my lawyer didn't really believe me, but he didn't want to tell my parents, so instead, he set up a test run. We paid $600 to take a private lie detector test before I was scheduled to take the real one. I had never taken one before, so I wasn't sure what to expect. First, the lady administering the test spent an hour or so talking to me about my life and who I was.

Then she said, "Ok, we're gonna take the lie detector test now."

She began with basic questions like, "Do you live in the United States?"

"What color is the sky?"

"Is it sunny outside?"

They use those questions as a baseline for whether or not you are telling the truth before they go into the actual questions.

They asked me many questions, and some were about things that I didn't know anything about. For example, they asked about the gun, where it came from, who it was connected to? They asked me if I had ever committed a robbery before, to which I replied, "no."

After the test was done, they came back in and told me that I passed. I think a lot about that first test, even today. I wonder whether or not I truly passed the test or if I just passed the lady's test because of who I was and my character. Maybe she concluded that the pending trial resulted from me having made some poor decisions and not me being who I truly was. The DA decided to accept that lie detector test instead of making me take another one.

With all of the support from the community and the passed lie detector test submitted to the courts, the DA recommended five years probation, with no jail time. The day after I finished my junior year of high school, we reported to court for formal sentencing. My parents stood behind me amidst an overly crowded courtroom. The same feelings of anxiousness that took over me the night we were arrested came back as I awaited Judge Aloi's final ruling.

And on that day, his words pierced our ears and my soul. He said, "Kwame, I can't forgive you for what you did."

I remember thinking to myself, it's not your role to forgive me as the judge. I can't recall if I said it aloud or not, but that weighed heavily on me. That almost stood out more to me than the sentencing at that moment. He said, "I can't forgive you." I thought, *are you, God? Is that your role, to forgive me for what I did?* What he said next came as even more of a shock to everyone in the courtroom that day.

"I can't forgive you, so I sentence you to one year."

The whole courtroom was speechless. The silence spoke so loud. Typically the judge accepts what the DA recommends. We were all planning for probation. I only expected to go back home after the sentencing. My parents and everyone else were planning for that because the DA had recommended it. We had gone through all these hurdles and garnered a ton of support to no end. We had no idea the judge was going to go against that.

From there, I was just numb. I couldn't feel anything after hearing that sentence. I wasn't expecting to go away for an entire year. For a seventeen-year-old, that felt like twenty years. Standing there in the courtroom, my summer and senior year began flashing through my head. My scholarships, my family, friends, and everything I worked for were all taken from me just like that. It felt like a lie. Like someone had messed up or that I was simply dreaming, but I wasn't. I was going to jail.

My mother and my sister broke down. They were yelling, screaming, and crying. My mom eventually walked out because it was too emotional for her to bear. I remember when they sat me down on the bench right before taking me away. I was sitting across from my father, and I looked at him with a haze in my eyes. It was surreal what was happening. Everyone else exited the courtroom, but my father stayed beside me. As he kept looking back at me, I could tell he, too, was getting emotional. He would not allow the pain in his eyes to fall as teardrops. He was holding it together for me. His face was reassurance that somehow, everything would be ok. My lawyer approached me, who came up and confirmed that we would reconvene to discuss everything that transpired later. There was such a shockwave sent throughout the courtroom that no one recognized we were not formally dismissed. As soon as court was adjourned, the bailiff put me in handcuffs and escorted me out of the courtroom. I was not given time to say goodbye to my family. It was the dreaded end to a tragic chapter and an uncertain beginning. My plan of attaining freedom at all costs backfired. I was now a captive, and freedom was yet a far cry.

To My Younger Self

If I could speak to my younger self, I would tell him three critical pieces of advice.

The first is to seek out mentors in the community to help you navigate through life's difficulties. You do not have to do it alone. There are people in your community who care and will help. The second piece of advice that I have for you is to never forget to ask for help. Too often, you see people who do not ask for help. There is help out there if you reach out to people, tell them what your problem is and what you need help with, but if you remain silent, you will isolate yourself from growth and realizing your potential. Lastly, build your confidence at all costs. To do anything phenomenal, you have to have confidence. Your confidence should not be based on what other people think of you; it should be a true reflection of how you feel about yourself internally.

What I Love Most

Spartan Race

Speaking at
Thomasville Elementary

Ernest Greer, Mayor Bottoms

4: CONVERSION

Pain is a more skilled teacher than pleasure.

|KJ|

WHEN SILENCE SPEAKS

After my sentencing, the bailiff secured handcuffs around my wrists before escorting me out of the courtroom. We traveled down a hallway towards an elevator that took us down into the courthouse's basement. Once outside, I was placed in a van with four other men, whom I'm sure were uncertain about their fate like me. I was the only minor. The van had tinted windows and bars on the outside. No one spoke, not even the police who escorted us. My assumption was that everyone was in shock and processing how life would change in their own way. We drove for approximately an hour. I was afraid because I didn't know what I would encounter. Then, for the first time on the entire trip, a man uttered a few words to me.

"Yeah man, this is Jamesville Correctional Facility. They've got a lot of people in this jail. They've got a program where you can get out in four months if you have good behavior or whatever."

His words gave me a glimmer of hope. In the state of New York, you have to do eighty percent of your sentenced time. So, of my year, I had to do a minimum of eight months with good behavior to get out in eight months, but based on what he said, it was possible that I could get out in half of that time if I played my cards right.

Just before being sentenced, I heard whispers about the Jamesville Correctional Facility. It was no secret that most of the guys in Jamesville were from the southside of Syracuse. And all I knew was that I was heading for the general population. I would be alone and left to deal with the same guys I sought the block's protection from when I was out. Would I have to fight to defend myself? Would they try to jump me? Would they even remember who I was? The medley of thoughts resulted from me trying to make sense of it all.

I also thought about Jorge. He went through the court process at the same time as I was, and initially, because he was on parole, they were going to recommend fifteen years for him. There was controversy around the decision.

Many questioned why he was getting fifteen, and I was only being recommended for probation. When they sentenced me to a year, they sentenced him to eight years. I heard about it from my lawyer later after the sentencing took place. We were never close friends; we were just people who had a similar pattern of thought regarding mischief. At that time, I was angry with him because I felt like he was the reason we got searched. Had I known he was on parole, things would have been different. At least, that is what I kept telling myself. At that moment, I blamed him for getting me jammed up. All I could think about was fear and anger. *How would I survive in a place filled with people from the southside, away from my family day and night?* On the bus ride, I was preparing myself to fight for my life in general population, but that's not where I ended up. In those last moments on the bus taking me away from the only life I'd known, I was only worried about the Southsiders I'd have to deal with. Yet, in reality, I was about to face something much worse, something I should've feared more. I was headed straight to solitary confinement.

UNTIL THE LESSON IS LEARNED, THE PROBLEM PREVAILS

The first stop when I arrived at Jamesville was processing. In processing, they interview you to see if you have any medical issues or if you are in a gang. They talked to me for close to three hours, trying their best to get the full analysis of who I was and what problems I might bring.

Next came the search. The guards at the prison make you take all your clothes off. They make you bend over and cough to make sure you're not trying to smuggle anything in. It's an intrusive and uncomfortable predicament. They take all your possessions and give you the clothes you'll be wearing for however long you are there. Every part of the old you is left in that room. Then they take you inside.

At that time in New York, there was a point system in place while you were in prison based on good behavior and the severity of your charges. Even though my record was sealed, I came into the Jamesville prison system with five felonies. Each felony carried points. The more violent the felony, the more points that felony carried. Much of this wasn't explained until sometime after they put me in the Hole. I had fifteen points on day one of my eight-month sentence, and I needed to be under ten to go into general population.

Straight from processing, the guards took me to the A unit. At Jamesville Correctional Facility, there were four different units, which were broken down by age and gender. The minor pod, which was C unit, I ended up there eventually; the women's unit which was all ages because they only had one pod, and the adult pod for men, which included ages nineteen and up. The A unit was solitary confinement; we called it The Hole.

The Hole was where you went if you had disciplinary problems, but it was also the first stop if you scored too high on the point system when you arrived. The Hole was a two-story row of cells organized into three blocks of five. I was on the second tier with five cells beneath me. In the Hole, small ventilation shafts connect all the cells in a block together, the ones both beside and below me. In A unit, you are in your cell twenty-three hours out of the day. I'll never forget the sounds and activity you could hear coming through those vents at any given hour. All the hope I had heading over to Jamesville on the bus ride diminished once they threw me in the Hole.

The Hole changed me in many ways, and it changed my perspective on a lot of things. I remember talking to a guy named Fifty. He was in the cell next to me for about ten days before he was gone. Everyone around me on the top floor came and went during my time up there.

Below me, there was a guy everyone called Too Tall; I never learned his real name. Too Tall was sentenced to a year at Jamesville for a minor marijuana charge. When we met, he was in his third year there. Too Tall was a lanky guy, standing at about six foot six. He had some long-standing mental health problems that manifested in many ways. Every night he was up, causing some sort of scene. One time he flooded his cell and started throwing feces at the guards. A lot of the other inmates would encourage him to cause a scene as their nightly entertainment. I always thought it was messed up the way they treated him.

Every time Too Tall started acting out, they'd assemble the SWAT team in full gear to kick in his door and extract him from his cell. The SWAT team would go in there, rough him up and haul him out. It was a loud and disruptive scene, and sometimes they'd even go as far as to spray him and his entire cell down with mace. The smell of mace and whatever Too Tall had been doing would waft up through the ventilation system and into my cell. They would set Too Tall up in a harness chair, butt naked in front of the entire A unit. He would scream and wail until the pain from the mace wore off, and then they would leave him there all night with no water. Throughout his four years in The Hole, Too Tall never got the help he needed. His mental health problems went completely unaddressed, and the cycle continued. I don't know what happened to Too Tall, but I will never forget the unjust way in which he was treated.

During the day, most of the inmates slept and were awake at night. That was how we dealt with doing time. Every night, the A unit would come alive with the noises of the inmates. We would communicate through the vents that connected our cells. Someone would drop a beat, and others would start rapping. You could hear the agony of new arrivals going through withdrawal.

One hour a day was devoted to being outside. It took place in a small fenced-in area, about twenty-by-twenty square feet, with a picnic table. They allowed three or four of us out at a time. We used the picnic table as weights. Bench pressing the table was the starting point. After that, people sat on the table as an added weight when you became strong enough. On some days, we talked and played cards. The hour went by quickly, and then you were ordered to go back into your cell. It was something to look forward to.

Music was a big part of getting us through that time at night. I was allowed to have my Walkman while there. I asked my parents to send me some music to play on my headset. I requested a few rap artists, DMX, Jay-Z, Capone and Noreiga, and one R&B group 112. The 112 album was the only one that got through. The jail confiscated all those other albums, likely because the content in the lyrics was too vulgar. 112 was the only album I had so I played it often. Later, when I got to general population, I also played the album in school. Much later in life, I had the opportunity to meet Q Parker from 112, and I told him how listening to his music during that time was one of the things that saved me. It was pretty special for me to share that with him. Today, we do a lot of work together to help young people.

In the Hole, my cell was next door to a guy named Anthony. He was from the south side of Syracuse, which meant that we were supposed to be enemies, but we weren't. We talked at night through the vent system about life. On some nights, we had these singing sessions, sometimes rapping together. Anthony had a habit of leaving and coming back to the A unit regularly. Every time he got into a fight, he would do ten days in the Hole.

I asked him once why he kept coming back to the Hole?

"Kwame," he said. "Your father comes to see you every week. My father is in the next unit, and I met him here for the first time."

His words hit me like a ton of bricks. I had two parents at home, and they worked hard to provide for my siblings and me. I was running track and even had a few scholarships lined up. I had a job at Wegmans. Even before I was convicted, I went to court and school like it was nothing. It was different for Anthony. When we went to chow, his father was a few units over. As we left lunch, he would walk right past him; they wouldn't even speak to each other.

I'll never forget that conversation because he was right. I missed my family. I missed my friends. I missed everybody, the life I had. Still, I had undeniable love even in my circumstance, which Anthony rightfully deserved but could not claim. Seeing my dad and the phone calls with some of my friends, including DJ and Lala, kept me grounded.

It took me almost two months to get low enough on the point system to qualify for general population. Once every two weeks, I met with a counselor named Dan, a real skinny, older white guy with glasses. Dan and I just talked. He would ask me how I was doing and inquire about what was going on with me? He gave me a lot of information regarding what it would be like doing time and resources if I needed them.

He started talking to me about the program the man on the bus told me about. He confirmed that I could get out in four months if I stayed out of trouble. Those four months seemed much more feasible to me than the entire sentence, so I put that on the forefront of my mind for the first few months. I can get out soon, I can do it, I thought to myself. I can do a little bit of time in solitary, do a couple of months in the general population, and then get out. I held onto that.

It was not until I hit the four-month mark that I learned my hope for an early release would not manifest. By that time, I was already halfway done with my sentence. I only had another four months to complete. Come to find out, the early release initiative was only for nonviolent offenses, and because I had a violent offense charge, I wasn't eligible for it from the start. Counselor Dan should have known that there was no way I would qualify. It is quite possible that he knew, but by sharing that information with me, he gave me a sense of hope that I would not have had otherwise.

In a twisted way, he was trying to help me. He wanted to get me through the first four months. At the four-month mark, he told me that I didn't qualify. It took almost two months to get my points low enough to be eligible for the general population. Looking back, it would have been a lot easier for me if they had put me in general population when I first arrived. I could have watched TV, gone out of my cell, seen and interacted with people, played basketball, or gone outside. It was my first time in jail outside of being arrested. Going straight to The Hole and A Unit was a shock to my system, and I experienced things that I'll never forget. Conversations and moments that stayed with me, even today. I was traumatized from it all, a sentiment that I would not wish upon my worst enemy.

HOPE IN GENERAL

I could see the C Unit from the fenced-in area outside of solitary confinement. Although it was far away, I could see people moving about and felt like I recognized some faces even at a distance. Since my first day in The Hole, I wanted to get to the general population. So when I finally got transferred, I had no regrets about leaving A Unit behind.

The C Unit was two tiers like solitary but much more open. There were about fifty cells throughout, twenty-five on each level. When I walked in, everyone else was coming out of their cells on the way to morning breakfast. I looked up at everyone as they passed, looking around the area and realized, everyone in there was from the southside. I was the only person in there from the east side. I'd met a few cool guys from the southside during my time in the Hole, but this was different. *What the hell is this about to mean for me?*

Eventually, I saw one dude, Darnell, from the east side. Although I didn't know him too well, he seemed like he had been able to adjust and fit in with all the guys from the southside. We were not supposed to like each other. We were supposed to hate each other, but that was out there on the streets. While we were locked up, we were all just trying to get through, do our time, and go home.

By the time I got situated in my cell, I could hear some of the guys making comments. Newbie, and freshman, were some of the ways they referenced me. I didn't pay it any mind, put my stuff down in my new cell, and got in line for chow with everyone else.

There was this white kid in line, and he might have been the only white person in the whole unit. He was in for molestation. It was rumored that he was there for molesting his sister. The other inmates were relentless, always giving him a hard time. They would slap him and rip his ID badge off. If you lost your ID badge, you were in trouble. They would rip his shirt and subject him through ongoing ridicule every time he would line up. It really stood out to me the way the other inmates treated him. It reminded me of the way they treated Too Tall. I don't remember if that kid ever got out, but I never participated in any of that kind of behavior.

Daily life in general population stayed on a set routine. You woke up, went to chow in the morning, and as a minor, you attended school. After a few hours of school, I played the 112 album. The teacher allowed us to do that during that time. We had a few different teachers that instructed us. After school, you went back to the cell, played basketball, or played cards just before lunch. The day ended with dinner. Day in and day out, that was the routine. At night you were locked down at nine o'clock. Before lockdown, at about seven o'clock, you could make phone calls. I would typically call my friend DJ and talk to him. I thanked his mom every time; her phone bill had to be a couple hundred bucks every month just by him talking to me. I also spoke to Lala. She was still my girlfriend at the time. My parents visited me on the weekends, so we didn't talk too much during the week.

There were two classes, the A group, and the B group. The A group kids weren't as far along as the kids in the B group, but their sole goal was to get you to pass the GED test. Upon arrival, you received a GED test. If you failed, they administered another one. In one day, you could take up to three tests. The irony was that they didn't teach you anything. If you took it enough times, you would start to remember the answers, and that's how they got you to pass your GED.

58

I told the officers that I wasn't going to take my GED and that I was going to get my diploma. Once I got out of the Hole and into general population, my track coach Maynord, came into the picture big time. Coach Maynord was my first mentor. He was a round white guy and stereotypically not what you would imagine as someone fighting relentlessly to mentor a convicted black boy from the streets of Syracuse, but he did. Coach Maynord had a heart of gold and believed in me. He visited me in prison and never allowed me to quit on myself.

I remember the first time he came to see me, sitting across from me in the visiting area.

"Kwame," Coach Maynord said. "We're going to get you through this. We're going to get you out of high school. You're going to graduate on time with your class, and we're going to get you a track scholarship."

I thought, how is that even possible? I'm here in jail, serving time for a violent crime. I've got to spend my entire senior year here, and you're talking about how I will graduate on time and get a track scholarship. But Coach Maynord didn't budge. He meant it. He put a plan in place, and we worked together as a team to execute.

We went to work. My parents and coach were a tag team for bringing my school work to me. The school agreed to the arrangement. The challenge was I didn't have any help, so I had to just kind of figure it out. The teachers weren't going to help me out with calculus or science or any other classes, so I'd sit on my bed going through math problems and homework questions until my head hurt and I could finally make sense of what I had to be doing. The school gave me the same assignments everyone else was doing. There was no room for easier homework just because I wasn't in the classroom. Somehow, someway, I figured it out. I ended up with a C in about every class at the end of the semester. Looking back, I don't know if they felt bad for me and just gave me the C for my effort, but I passed. The people around me who refused to give up on me inspired me to not give up on myself. My gratitude to those that helped me during that time can't be put into words.

Aside from my parents and Coach Maynord, there were others who were instrumental in my education while in prison, such as Allen Rosenthal and Marsha Weissman. These souls have become some of my greatest inspirations for the way I mentor today. Coach Maynord believed in me when so many teachers and community members had given up on me. So many people chalked me up to be just another product of my environment. Despite not being able to control or change my environment, they decided that it was my fault, and that's just how I was going to be. Coach Maynord saw the potential within me. He saw the scared young boy that needed guidance, and he became it. My friends and family who supported me, and even those I met in prison that supported me like Anthony from the southside, all aided me in discovering my light. These people and the lessons I learned from each of them have allowed me to mentor relentlessly today. We all need mentors who can guide us and help us discover the hope inside. It is precisely what saved me.

Speaker at ATL Rotary

Family

Leadership ATL class
at Falcons Game

Brown Middle School

Fulton County Commissioner
Robb Pitts

Day One Friends

5: Adjustment

Never Forget That The End Is The Beginning.

|KJ|

"Kwame, get out of this situation."

In addition to pursuing my high school diploma, I decided to work in the kitchen. Now, in general population, things are going well with the continued support of Coach Maynord and my parents. Still, I wanted to get out of the unit. Chances were that if you stayed in the unit, you were going to get into trouble.

The minor unit, also known as the C unit, saw the most violence out of all the units at Jamesville. People were gambling and fighting, it was very easy to get roped into that and the negative stuff going on in the unit. The adult units were much calmer and less violent, so I started working in the kitchen for breakfast. Over time, I started working all the shifts available breakfast, lunch, and dinner.

I spent most of my time between school and the kitchen, and I really enjoyed it. I got to be around older guys whose company taught me significantly. I got to hear their stories, and these guys had significant convictions and served a great deal of time in prison during their lives. Some of them were down for murder, did twenty years, got back in trouble, and did a little stint in Jamesville. There was one guy who had all these exotic animals. He made national news while in possession of tigers and peacocks, and he got in trouble for doing that. There was also this gay guy named Boo Boo who was super cool, and he braided everyone's hair. He was a booster; he got in trouble for stealing clothes. That was his profession. All these tough guys went to Boo Boo, sat between his legs, and let him braid their hair before their visits. A collection of different people that just, somehow, worked well together, and I was becoming a part of that.

I started off in the kitchen washing dishes and eventually worked my way to the line. This was significant because, in jail, food is essential, and if you don't have a commissary and people don't send you money, you rely on those three meals a day. Over time, I eventually worked my way up to be the lead, the head person on the line to serve the main course. I would serve the chicken if we had chicken, vegetables, and rice. I determined how much the portion sizes were. I was always very generous with the scoop sizes, which gave me a lot of notoriety and respect in the jail. It's kind of crazy that it even matters, but it does. People appreciated just that little gesture of extra food on their plate. I was the only minor that ever became a line cook, let alone the lead.

I spent a little bit of time with the Muslim brothers at Jamesville. My father converted to Islam when I was in middle school, so I used to go to the mosque, and then I would go to church with my mom on Sundays. Still, to this day, my mom is a Christian, and my dad is a Muslim, and they coexist, which is something special. Their relationship taught me a lot about religion and marriage. I participated in Ramadan, and during fast, I would deliver meals which enabled me to go into some of the adult units. I was able to move throughout the whole prison during Ramadan. I remember being close to the Muslim brothers because they are nonviolent and structured. During those thirty days, the small sense of community and brotherhood was a breath of fresh air.

They were all supportive of me finishing my degree. You would think that in prison, me doing my schoolwork would be frowned upon or criticized, but it was not. Even the corrections officer responsible for oversight of the kitchen kept me encouraged. There were one or two people— I could count them on my hand— that weren't supportive, but they were not impactful enough to make a difference.

"Do your homework, Kwame," they said. "Get yourself out of here."

They believed in me, and for that, I was thankful.

Life Is A Powerful Teacher

There were too many nights I spent lying awake in jail to count. It is hard to process the thoughts of loved ones and the world outside of the prison walls that are moving forward without you. There were nights when I could not sleep, so I spent the time listening to the radio and hearing about what was going on in the city. In the stillness and silence, every noise was amplified. The nighttime forced you to deal with the reality of being in jail.

For every good person encountered, there was no denying that several corrections officers working at Jamesville were not the best people. Depending on which CO you're dealing with, you likely encountered racism. They entertained themselves by playing games with the inmates. When they locked you down, they would throw you in your cell and hurl slurs and insults at you while saying things to make your already hard life harder.

The other aspect of prison that no one speaks about is pain. Having to navigate the various dynamics and personalities of scores of young men who not only have their own sets of issues but those who are locked up in a confined space. This dynamic results in conflict and turmoil. There was always some type of beef over simple things like card games or basketball. The truth is that everyone inside was hurting. Prison is an incubator for pain. And because most inmates are not well-versed in when, where, and how to channel the pain, people hurt one another. The weight of navigating and surviving this dynamic day in and day out is challenging. My goal was to not get caught up in fights or conflicts. Doing so meant ten days in the Hole.

Some people that went into the Hole never came back the same. We had all seen it with a guy from my own neighborhood, Darnell. Darnell got in a fight with some guys from the southside, so they put him in the Hole for ten days. When he came back, he was a completely different person. He was talking to himself and taking medicine. In the following days, they shipped him off to a mental institution. To this day, I'm told Darnell never fully recovered.

Due to the mounting frustrations, fights were not easily avoided. The one time I had a fight issue, it happened to be with someone from my neighborhood. A guy named Knowledge came into the general population about a month after me. By this time, Darnell was already gone, and I was the only kid from the eastside in C unit. I knew what Knowledge was going through, being new, not knowing anybody, and being from the eastside like me. I knew the other inmates would give him a hard time for a little while, so I helped him out. When he came in, all he had were the flip-flops and the clothes they gave him at processing. I gave him some food, took him around, and told everybody that he was cool to ease off and leave him alone.

Unbeknownst to me, someone went into my cell and stole all my stuff. It was a normal thing at Jamesville, but it didn't make it right. People would wait for you to leave and then steal your commissary, food, and anything else of value when you were not looking. It didn't take me long to find out that Knowledge, of all people, took my stuff out of my cell. Once I learned that he was responsible, I walked down to his cell to confront him. Everyone in the C unit was following me because they could sense that there was about to be a fight.

Luckily, the CO on duty at the time was watching what was going on. He came down and got between us and broke the potential commotion before it went too far. They usually don't even bother to help. In most instances, they would lock the entire unit down even though Knowledge and I hadn't come to blows yet and send us both to the Hole for ten days. A scenario like this would have been detrimental for me because I had successfully served so much of my time. I think that CO felt sorry for me and knew Knowledge was wrong, so he prevented the whole thing from happening.

5: ADJUSTMENT

My parents visited every weekend to see how I was doing. They collected my homework and talked for as long as possible. Every time I went into the visitation room to see my parents, the guards strip-searched me. I hated going through that. The experience of being strip-searched and someone telling you to bend over and spread it was so humiliating and violating for me. Every time you leave the visit you have to do that. I loved seeing my parents, so I went through it, but the experience was awful. Seeing my parents through the glass was the best part of the week at Jamesville. My parents usually came by themselves. They never let my younger siblings Jamal and Jamila see me in prison. My older sister Karrish and my brother Oliver were both off in college and other places, but Jamal and Jamila were at home when I got arrested and went to Jamesville.

The most challenging day for me in jail was the one time they broke their rule of allowing my younger siblings to visit. This time, they brought Jamal to see me. It was towards the end of my sentence, and I knew I didn't have long until I was out, but I'll never forget the look on his face. It was one of confusion. Looking back, it was a good thing that he got to see me like that, so he could learn from my mistakes and never end up in a situation like that. Outside of being in the Hole, dealing with the staff and the Knowledge situation, that day was one of the worst. I felt like I had let him down. The expression on his face was confirmation that I did.

FAILURE IS NOT AN OPTION

Just shy of my eighth month in prison, I was doing calculus on my own. My plan was to get out by February and enroll in night school, day school, and summer school to graduate on time with my class in June. The next goal was to attain eligibility for an NCAA track scholarship. Once again, Coach Maynord went to work for me. He continued to recruit for me, and eventually, Hampton University decided to give me a shot. They were willing to award me a partial scholarship if I got out of jail and stayed out of trouble. At that time in 2001, you had to score at least an 800 on your SATs to be eligible for an NCAA track scholarship. I had never taken the test before, and I would inevitably be in jail during the test period. The challenge was to figure out how I could participate in the testing while incarcerated.

With approximately two months left to go home, I learned that I could apply for a furlough. A furlough is different in different places. In some places, it allows you to go home and work, or it could be used to attend a funeral. Where I was, a furlough enabled you to go home for twenty-four hours if approved during your last two months. Most people would take their furlough, go home, get high, get drunk, and have sex. And when they returned, they would sleep the next two months of their time away. Prison was hard, so I recognized that guys were in need of reprieve. I just had a little something different in mind for how I would put my furlough to use.

Everyone that I knew who applied was approved even if they had been in fights before. As long as you weren't in trouble at the time of your two-month mark, access was granted.

To get your furlough approved, you had to go in front of five members of the Jamesville faculty. The warden was also present, and they would review your file and either approve or disapprove of you. There was no application process, only the thirty-minute interview. Since I needed to take my SATs, my parents and I requested my furlough be granted not to go home but to go to a testing site to have the test administered. We requested that I get six hours—not even the full twenty-four— to go to my high school and then return. We presented our case to the review board. We spoke about me doing my schoolwork, working in the kitchen, mentoring other inmates, and the fact that I had college offers and a track scholarship pending. I spoke openly about my mistakes and how I wanted to make good on those poor choices. The last piece needed to get my life started on the right path was to take my SATs. After I pleaded my case, the faculty left the room to discuss. When they reentered, the speaker looked at me and told me that they were denying my furlough. They stated that they believed me to be a threat to society.

I pleaded, "If I take my SATs and go to college, I'll be less of a threat to society." They denied it anyway.

I was devastated. We were all working so hard, and it appeared that our efforts went unrecognized. I left the meeting and went back to my cell while accepting that I would be forced to wait until the following year to make good on any of my hopes and aspirations.

My cell was filled with booklets and reading materials that I read every day to prepare for the test. I sat down on the floor and picked up the SAT college board booklet. Flipping through the book randomly brought a sick feeling to my stomach. I was crushed at the moment. Amidst my feelings of hopelessness, a section in the book caught my eye. There was a section that spoke about accommodations for disabled students. According to the pamphlet, if you have a disability and can't make it to a testing site, they would administer the test on-site. Essentially, they would bring the SAT to you. The pamphlet prompted me to contact the college board to obtain more information. I immediately picked up my pen, grabbed a piece of paper, and wrote them a letter. In the letter, I explained where I was located and that I couldn't get to a test site; therefore, I had a disability. They wrote back with an approval for the test to be administered on-site at Jamesville. And although their approval of the test being brought to me was a win, it caused turmoil in the jail.

The warden stated that it had not been done before and that they were leary of executing a new procedure of this magnitude.

I looked at him and said, "Listen, if you make this a problem, my parents and I are going to go to the press, and we are going to say that you are trying to hold me back. This is supposed to be about rehabilitation. There is no reason to withhold the testing option from me."

Needless to say, I was approved. Not only had the college entrance exam never been administered at Jamesville, but it had never been administered in prison in the United States. I would be the first. The night before I was to take my exam, I can remember studying and working like never before. My nerves worked overtime, but I had been preparing, and in my heart, I knew that I was ready.

Early the next morning, the day of my exam, they told us that they wanted to do a shakedown of the unit. The whole time I had been there, I had never been through a shakedown. They never demanded to search all of the rooms, but for some reason, on that day, of all days, they did.

During a shakedown, they ask you to go outside of your cell and wait while they practically turn your room upside down. We're all standing on the balcony while they search our cells. I was anxiously waiting for them to be done, but I was not worried about it. I knew they would not find anything in my cell worth discovering. When the corrections officer came out of my cell, he held a cigarette up in his hand. Cigarettes are contraband in prison. Possession of one gets you ten days in the Hole.

I felt my heart racing as I maintained my composure. Maybe it was a mistake, I thought to myself. I knew the cigarette did not belong to me. There is no way that I would have risked getting caught with something like that so close to my exam.

The guard looked at me and asked, "Is this your cigarette son?"

"No, I don't even smoke," I replied.

"Well, this was in your cell, so we got to take you to the Hole," he said.

I knew that I couldn't take my test if I went to the Hole. In my head, this was all intentional. Somebody planted the cigarette there in an attempt to prevent me from taking my test. I was terrified. I had worked so hard and that cigarette in the guard's hand meant destruction for all of my efforts.

Before my heart could explode, I heard a voice from behind me.

"That's mine," it said.

My friend Shank stepped forward. We met as enemies. He was from the southside, and we were never meant to be friends, but during our time in Jamesville, we were on good terms. He stepped forward and told those guards that the cigarette was his. They put Shank in the Hole after that. He was willing to risk his sanity so I could take my test.

And on that day, it was because of Shank that I had an opportunity to make good on my promise to my parents,

Coach Maynord, and myself. I took the test and passed with flying colors. I will never forget the sacrifice Shank made for me. Without that moment, I can honestly say that I don't know what the future would have held for me.

NEVER FORGET US

The night that I was released was a whirlwind. Since I had never been in trouble when I was there, they allowed me to leave at midnight instead of ten in the morning. That meant I had twelve hours off my sentence for good behavior. Typically everyone is asleep at this time, but as I walked past cells, I noticed some of the guys awake and peering out. I could see their eyes looking out of the small windows on the doors of each of their cells. Then, to my surprise, I heard them clapping. They were giving me a round of applause. The subtle claps turned into roars and cheering.

They begin shouting out, "Kwame, never forget us!" and "Kwame, go as far as you can go!"

Their words were like melodies to my heart. Here were the kids that society said to throw away, cheering for someone who had been granted a second chance. Amidst those cheers was the spirit of hope and goodness. Some were still holding out on the prospect of their own second chance, and others had come to the reality that prison was their final destination. Their words confirmed that they thought I was supposed to have a different life even though we grew up in the same city and, in some cases, the same side of town. These sentiments carry me as I work to make a difference today. The task they gave me was not to forget them and go as far as I could. I have carried this energy with me since I was seventeen. I have never forgotten them, and I never will. From that moment forward, my mission became to go as far as I could for all the guys at Jamesville who believed in the person I was back then and my potential to become the person I am today.

6: SHIFT

Freedom must not be assumed.
Therefore, it is won.

|KJ|

No Turning Back

Three to four feet of snow rested on the ground when I was released from prison in the middle of a harsh New York winter. I'll never forget the sound of the ice beneath my shoes when I stepped out of the prison doors in the middle of the night. And although I was excited to be out, I was also nervous. It had been so long since I experienced freedom. Even the feeling of the air across my skin was different. Today, I still can't describe the welling up of emotions that took over me when I realized that I was standing on the other side of the fence that held me captive.

My parents were there to pick me up and take me home. We didn't talk on the ride home. I was still in a state of shock. It felt surreal knowing that I no longer had to be subjected to endless fights, kitchen duty, correctional officers, or scrutiny.

When we arrived home, I quickly overcame the awkwardness I felt stepping back into the house for the first time in eight months. The first thing I did was go into the kitchen, reach in the refrigerator, and I grabbed a coke soda. It was the first time I had a soda since I'd been sentenced. It felt like a shot of liquor.

In my room, everything felt small. Even though it was much bigger than my sleeping quarters in jail, it felt like I was in a miniature space. It now felt foreign and strange to me, but eventually, I settled in. I showered and laid awake for a little while in my bed. By the time I got comfortable enough to sleep, I had stayed there for what felt like a few days.

When I awoke, I set my intentions towards trying to get back into school to finish out the last few months of my senior year. I wanted nothing more than to graduate with my class.

Later, I learned that my little sister Jamila had been working on a petition to get me back into school. She had gone around campus with a piece of paper asking folks to sign off on it. Her efforts were not in vain. She eventually acquired enough signatures and support to grant me reentry.

On my first day back, I recognized how my time at Jamesville changed me. Before going to prison, I was clean-cut. I wore a sharp fade, and my clothes were neat. After eight months in jail, my hair had grown out, and I was still rocking Boo Boo's braids. I kept the braids for about two weeks before cutting them off. I wanted to go back to who I was before assimilating in the streets and prison. Another aspect of rediscovering myself was trying out for the track team. Doing so was not as easy as I assumed it would be. My body was different. When I went into jail, I weighed about 140-145lbs. I mainly was lean muscle. In prison, the food, lack of exercise, and activity in jail meant I'd put on about twenty-five pounds more. The extra weight was significant as a competitor in the four hundred. In spite of it all, I found a way to push through. There were only a few meets for me to compete in, yet we still made it to state. I ran the four-by-four, but admittedly, I was never as fast as I was before jail, and that carried on into college.

While in prison, I attended day school and night school. The only class I could not complete was gym class. Once I was released, there were no night classes for gym at my school, so we went to another high school in my town. There were around a hundred kids assigned to the class. There was no real structure for the course. They instructed us to walk around the track, and that was gym at night. If walking around the track was what it took for me to graduate on time, then so be it.

I was fighting to get back to the life I had once known despite it all. Lala and I were back to spending time together and even traveling to track meets out of town. Later, I learned that she had been cheating on me with some other guy for a while. To make matters worse, someone had seen her driving him around in my car. Where we were from, that was the ultimate sign of disrespect. When I confronted her about it, she admitted to everything. That was the break that ended our relationship. My heart was shattered. She helped me get through such a difficult time, including trial and prison. She was my emotional support in addition to my friend named DJ. Never would I have imagined that Lala would betray me like that. A part of me understood because I was away and couldn't be there for her like she needed me to be. I was forced to deal with the hurt from the break-up and the mounting pressure of finishing school my only direction was through.

Pomp and Circumstance

The weight of my plight to race the clock to graduate on time, coupled with my first heartbreak, was heavy. I kept going until everything I worked for throughout the trial, jail, and the tumultuous testing scenario manifested. With grace and mercy in my favor, I was able to graduate high school on time with my class, a day I thought I might never see, but I did. I resolved to never allow anyone or anything, including myself, to stand in the way of my future and the potential placed upon my life ever again. From that point forward, my motto became by any means necessary. I vowed to dream bigger than I ever had. I dedicated myself to personifying the proof of the value that others placed upon me, regardless of whether or not I demonstrated the same level of value for myself. It was time to write a new chapter.

On the day of graduation, I remember putting on my cap and gown, looking in the mirror, and thinking about the road I had taken to get here. Quitting basketball and starting track, the robbery, arrest, the trial, and all of the tribulations amidst what felt like the hardest eight months of my life in prison. Yet, I overcame everything I'd been through. That day, I felt like I had officially made it.

While standing in line waiting to receive my diploma, my nerves attempted to get the best of me. I could feel myself fidgeting, and I was unsure of how the crowd would react when I walked on stage. No one thought I would get out of jail any time soon, let alone graduate from high school with my class.

When I heard my name called, I stepped on stage and just put one foot in front of the other. Looking up to see my mom standing there, smiling at me, with tears in her eyes, filled my heart with unexplainable joy. Little did I know they would call my mom onto the stage to give me my diploma. Her presence reminded me to hold my head up slightly higher and stand a little taller as I walked towards her. Like the inmates had done for me, watching me as I walked toward my future, the crowd cheered for me. They cheered as my mom handed me my diploma. I defied the odds to feel a single sheet of paper rolled like a scroll in my hands. As we embraced on stage, I could not hold back the tears, so I allowed them to flow freely.

I was off to pre-college at Hampton University less than two weeks later. We packed up the minivan with a final destination of Hampton, Virginia. Not only had I never been to Hampton, but I had also never toured the campus, but they accepted me, and I was enrolled. That was all that mattered to me.

Hampton University is a historically black college near Virginia beach. It was amazing driving up there and seeing the glittering ocean right before our eyes. It is a beautiful campus on the water. "Home by the Sea" is their slogan.

The school was vastly different from the units at Jamesville, crammed in quarters with only men in sight. At Hampton University, there were approximately 7,000 students, and only 500 of them were men. There were two men's dorms, and the rest were for women. It was an environment I had never experienced before, yet eager to explore.

My parents stayed a few hours to get me situated before departing. We transferred all of my belongings from the car and put them in my dorm. I checked in, attended to financial aid and other administrative tasks required of freshmen. When it came time for my parents to leave, my mom was hesitant. She was crying and hugging me so tightly that my father had to pull her away.

"We got him here." He spoke his peace, and before I knew it, they were gone.

From that day forward, everything moved rapidly. Going from jail to graduation was very dramatic and now I've added a college campus to the mix. It was only a matter of weeks since my release, and there I was in another state away from my family and friends. I didn't know a soul when I arrived at Hampton, but I was a survivor. I would eventually figure it out.

Attending track practice every day was an open door to forge new relationships. Over time, I made some friends on the team. We were all conveniently on the same floor of our dorm. Harkness Hall became the stomping ground, and we did everything together. We had lunch together, dinner together, and we most often went to practice together. The first day of practice was overwhelming for me. They had us warm up with a five-mile run. I didn't have the same level of training back in Syracuse. We didn't run that much; we were all surviving off of natural talent. We didn't even have a proper track to practice on; it was just rocks and dirt.

My transition to a division one track program, twenty-five pounds heavier than in high school, proved challenging. I was now running with men from Texas, South Carolina, and Florida. They ran year-round in much warmer climates than upstate New York. Needless to say, things intensified for me. My body was not ready, and I also discovered that I was not mentally prepared. There was no question that I had natural ability, which allowed me to keep up with everyone else, but the battle was hard-won. Track became an enormous task mentally for me. It wasn't fun anymore. We were never there on the weekends, so I never got to experience college the way I really wanted to.

A few months into the track program at Hampton, I was on the fence, wondering if I had made the right decision. Since my scholarship was only partial, I was not getting all the money I needed for school. So I went to my coach, Coach Boyd, to see if anything could be done.

I went to him and said, "Coach Boyd man, I want to tell you what happened to me before I got here. I don't know if you know."

He said he didn't, so I told him.

"I don't feel like I'm meeting the obligation and the commitment to the scholarship, so I want to give that back," I said. "I'm just going to work with financial aid instead. I'm going to work at Red Lobster and figure it out."

He paused for a moment, then looked at me and said, "Kwame you can do it. You've got all this talent. I know you've been through a tough patch, and it's going to take some time to get to where you want to be, but I want to tell you one thing, and I don't want you to ever forget it: Once you quit one thing, it's always easier to quit something else."

As I've gone through life, I've always remembered that. Once you develop a quitting mindset, it applies to all parts of your life. I placed great value on the notion of not quitting. Moving on from something is different, but quitting is a lack of discipline and self-control. This was a lesson learned much later in life. I moved forward with my decision to quit track. I never wanted to be a quitter, not after everything I'd been through, but this was becoming less and less worth it to me. I no longer saw the benefit in the work and energy I was exercising.

My decision was not a wise choice. After I quit track, I fell further and further into a cycle of hanging out and partying. I was at the student center every day and in the yard every day. Sleeping in, skipping class, chasing girls, and partying all weekend became my new normal. The only real productive thing I did was work at Red Lobster. Those behaviors caught up with me, and by the end of my first semester at Hampton, I was on academic probation.

There were about thirty of us on academic probation. They brought us all into a room and told us that things were about to change going forward. They changed our schedules. We were no longer able to take twelve credits per semester. We still had to pay tuition for eighteen credits but couldn't take the total amount of classes needed. They didn't assign us a mentor or coach. We were just told to do better in school.

It didn't feel like a supportive program at all. There wasn't anything to address why someone might be struggling or not doing well in school. It is my hope that they now have better support programs to help those who may be struggling in college. That is something I focus on a lot now in my work because many students I went to school with never actually made it out. I witnessed many of my friends, particularly men, drop out during freshman year, and some were on academic probation. There was no safety net.

Coming into Hampton University was such a hard transition for me, going from an all-male environment to a primarily woman-dominated environment. After living with only men, I was easily distracted by all of the women there, and it probably wasn't the best environment for me. It was also a hard transition coming from jail, a scheduled and regulated environment, to college, where I was in charge of myself. All of these things added up, and I ended up in a place academically that was not favorable.

The job at Red Lobster was the only place where I performed up to the required standards. I started out as a dishwasher like I did at Jamesville and eventually became the fry guy. I would fry all the food at Red Lobster and work my way up to the headline cook. It was good money, so I increased my hours until I worked more than going to school. By the end of my freshman year, my grades were worse. I was living life more like an adult instead of a student at that point. The path and pursuit of my initial goals before arriving at college slowly faded away.

POETIC JUSTICE

Although school was not going according to plan, my personal life was prospering. Just before the summer of my freshman year, I attended what we referred to as a sweatbox party. They were hosted in the gym, and hundreds of people would attend. They would switch the lights off, and everyone would cram together, dancing with no AC and not a care in the world. Everyone would be sweating and pushing against one another. It was there that I met Tanya.

With very little consideration for the fact that I was inebriated, I walked up to her and initiated a conversation. Tanya was a private school girl out of DC. Because of her father's work, she grew up around politics and activism, so the sweatbox party was not really Tanya's scene. She stood out to me more because she appeared to be different from many of the other girls at the party. The more I learned, the more I was intrigued. She wasn't like any girl I had met before. As a straight-A student, she was in the honors program and had come from a wealthy family. I didn't expect her to be into a guy like me from New York, who was hanging out wearing Timberlands and white t-shirts. Truth be told, I was still carrying a lot of old habits. Those same habits were to blame for my lack of success at Hampton.

Despite our differences, or maybe because of them, Tanya and I connected. She gave me her room extension—back in those days, they'd give you the last four digits of your dorm room number. I don't recall writing it down, but somehow, I remembered the numbers the next day despite all the alcohol I had consumed. She came into my life for a reason. After I called, we ended up hanging out. We got really deep in a short period of time, and not long after we met, we were in an exclusive relationship.

Summer break came around, and I had no desire to return home. I also didn't want to stay at Hampton because everyone else had plans to leave. I remember talking to Tanya about my summer plans.

"At least come up to DC," she said. "Meet my family, and then you can keep driving up to Syracuse and go home."

Her offer was music to my ears. Tanya and I drove up to her home in Silver Springs, Maryland. Silver Springs is an affluent part of the DC area. Tanya's family's home was situated in a picturesque neighborhood with massive houses. Admittedly, I was a little starstruck when we got there. It was my first time being in a neighborhood of this caliber. As we were waiting in the parking lot just outside the home, Bob Woodson pulled up in a brand new Jaguar.

Bob Woodson, a conservative community leader, civil rights activist, and Tanya's father. Bob split from the mainstream civil rights movement because he thought their work benefited middle-class blacks and not those who were poor and disenfranchised. He built himself up as the conservative Jesse Jackson if you can picture a conservative Jesse Jackson. That's a joke but the way I describe Bob sometimes.

One thing that always stood out to me when I saw Bob for the first time was the license plate on his car. He had the dealer advertisement around his plate, and it said Rosenthal, which was the name of my lawyer. I don't think there was any connection, but it was weird to me, and I've never forgotten that.

Bob took us out to a Mexican restaurant and insisted on paying for everything. He talked with me a lot about the work that he was doing around the country with community leaders to reduce gangs and violence. Tanya knew my story by this point, but I wasn't ready to share that with Bob just yet. I spent a couple of nights in Silver Springs with them before making my way to Syracuse.

The entire time I was in Syracuse, I couldn't stop thinking about Tanya and how I needed to get back to Maryland to be with her. Spending time in Syracuse was not a good idea for me, considering the history of my life there and all that I had been through. I made the decision to go back to Hampton to complete summer school. Whether or not I admitted it at the time, they weren't going to allow me back in the fall if I didn't get my grades back in order. Between summer school and Red Lobster, I traveled on as many weekends as I could to DC to see Tanya.

By sophomore year at Hampton, I was still not performing well academically. When fall semester finals were administered, I was fishing or at Virginia beach instead of showing up to class. That semester Hampton University wrote me a letter. They were officially dismissing me from the university. To this day, I have never disclosed to my parents that Hampton kicked me out. After reading the letter, I didn't know what to do. Returning to Syracuse was not an option, but it didn't feel like my life was making any forward progression. I remember sitting down with Tanya and talking about it.

"You should write my father a letter." she said, "You've got a powerful story, and he does that kind of work. Write to him, see what he says."

After pondering her offer, I decided to go for it. I sat down and wrote him a letter that ended up being around four pages long. A letter that he still has to this day. I told him my story, what I was going through and that I really respected the work he was doing to build up communities from the inside out all over the country. I told him that I would love to be a part of that if he thought there was a part for me to play.

Bob Woodson not only wrote me back but also asked me to come up to DC to talk with his vice president, Terence Mathis—another big player in my life—and interview with him. I was still driving the same car I had since high school, with speakers and no AC, which wasn't a problem in the north, but definitely a problem in the south. I stopped by Walmart and Payless right before the interview to get a pair of nice shoes and slacks.

After speaking with Terence, they decided to give me a job. I didn't ask about salary or what I would be doing; it did not matter. I was nineteen years old, and I was glad to have another chance to right my wrongs.

They immediately put me to work in the Violence Free Zone program. The program was focused on violence prevention and mentoring, emphasizing deterring kids from joining gangs in their areas. When I arrived at the building to which I was assigned, I was greeted by a lady named Ms. Amy, and I was given a salary of $30,000 a year. My role was that of a program assistant. At the time, I didn't realize that $30,000 was not a lot of money, especially in DC. In addition, the offer came with a single requirement for me to finish my degree.

After relocating to DC, I enrolled at the University of Maryland. They offered to pay for my degree if I attended classes at night. I never returned to Hampton after that. Before I moved to DC, I had to tell my parents. I called them and told them that things were not working out at Hampton. I didn't tell them that I had gotten kicked out. I went on to explain that Bob was offering me a job in DC, and I would go to school up there. They disagreed with my decision. They wanted me to stay at Hampton and finish school there, but I moved anyway. There are times when you have to listen to wise counsel, and there are times when you have to be led by your inner GPS. I chose the latter.

7: Revision

*We are in the greatest danger when
we resolve to fight evolution.*

|KJ|

Relationships Over Everything

My new role was as a program assistant at the Woodsen Center, formally known as the Center for Neighborhood Enterprise—which consisted of doing the little odd-end tasks around the office. The sole mission of CNE was to help residents of low-income neighborhoods address the problems in their communities. Whatever Bob and Terence wanted me to do or needed to be done, I did it. From attending meetings and setting up the projectors to ensuring the technology was working, and all the printouts were present, I made sure things were the way they needed to be. Bob and Terence weren't good with projectors, and back in those days, there was always an issue with technology. So I became an expert.

Their meetings were a training ground for leadership. I put extra care and time into everything I did. And while in those meetings, I was able to be a fly on the wall, listening and learning from the important conversations taking place. I learned a lot being in that role, and it's become something I stress now all the time. It doesn't matter what your job is or what it's like; make the best out of it. Learn everything you can, soak up everything you can. I made the best out of that job and benefited from it in so many ways, just by working the projector.

At first, it was a huge shock for me to be included in Bob's world. I would spend time at their house, visit their summer house on Virginia Beach and experience the energy of Washington, DC. I got a lot of exposure to a way of life I wasn't familiar with.

The office was located on 16th and K Street in the NW, blocks near the White House. On a daily basis, I ventured out into the city and ate my lunch outside the White House. During that time, I saw everyone in crisp suits, going about their business and doing what appeared to be important work. Now at the age of twenty-one, I appreciated the consistency necessary to build a real life, free from trial and tribulation that was self-inflicted. I also recognized that the energy of DC was like nothing I had experienced. As a result, I began to think differently, and the change of mindset exposed me to a new way of living.

My hard work and diligence were paying off. I eventually got promoted to Program Manager, and then ultimately Director. Bob, Terence, and I became a trio, working closely together. I was Bob's number three, Terence was his number two, and I reported directly to him. Over the following seven years of being there, I worked with Bob and Terence one on one. I learned so much from them about leadership, professionalism, and confidence. A lot of black people are not confident in their own skin because of their experiences and sometimes lack thereof. There are times when we are afraid to share our stories for fear of being judged or misunderstood. We are conditioned not to recognize the power in our stories.

Bob and Terence showed me that it was ok to have mistakes in your past and that you can still be a leader and be seen as a leader despite them, perhaps even because of them. In this position, my fundamental base as a professional was established.

Bob was well connected throughout DC, particularly with conservatives. He brought me to the White House, and we met with George Bush Jr., who was president at that time. Their example showed me how to be confident and be in those rooms with the movers and shakers, which is half the battle, especially for black leaders.

The art of building relationships was another aspect of what Bob taught me. He took me around the world. I met people from every walk of life, from former drug dealers and gang bangers to presidents, dignitaries, and esteemed dignitaries like Colin Powell and Clarence Page. Bob also introduced me to a ton of celebrities. I watched in the wings and learned his strategy for building relationships. Today, I recognize that relationships are the core necessity for any leader to succeed. I also learned that relationships change people, not programs.

THE CHANGEMAKERS

The bandwidth of my responsibilities at CNE increased. My new responsibilities included working with local leaders around the country who had experience in the prison system and those who wanted to make a change in their communities. As the Program Manager, I oversaw the Violence Free Zone program. We hired ex-gang members, teen moms, etc., trained them, and deployed them into schools to prevent other kids from assimilating with gangs. I traveled all over the country, raising money and bringing visibility to our work. Our work was not mainstream, and schools wouldn't typically let people with these backgrounds in their buildings, but through our results, reputations and relationships cultivated, we convinced superintendents and principals to serve in this capacity. The real proof was our ability to be impactful in many of the most challenging schools.

Even though I managed great responsibility, I was only twenty-one at the time. There were times when the company had to get approval for me to secure rental cars to drive around the various cities and states to do my work. The program was growing, and I was excelling. This role, in particular, helped me discover my passion and I was pouring myself into the work. My personal story was directly tied to the advocacy that had now become my life's mission. The Violence Free Zone program exposed me to so many change-makers and influential people, many of whom were a part of smaller organizations. Coming up close and personal with leaders who were doing the groundwork in schools and communities and those who had not received the attention mattered most to me. These individuals were about real impact, and that mat-tered most.

During one of my assignments, I traveled to Dallas and met Antong Lucky. Antong founded a Bloods chapter in Dallas and went to prison for many years. During his time in prison, he met so many young men who were coming in with life sentences. Teenagers with life sentences. He told me that he felt responsible because these young people said to him that they had put it down for Blood. So he changed his life in prison and began mentoring the young men in the prison system. Once out of prison, he recruited six or seven other young men and women, and they went into Madison High School, where he attended school. At the time, the school had proven to be extremely challenging. They reported hundreds of violent incidents every year. Fifty sixty or so kids walking the hall every period was normal. No education was happening because of the violence until Antong Lucky went in. In addition to his team, he recruited some changemakers from a rival gang, the Crips. More specifically, a guy named Gover, who was once a Crip leader. These guys were not supposed to work together, but they went into Madison High School and created immeasurable change in just one year. That school went from being notoriously violent, having the cops parked outside every day, or coming inside the school every day at lunch to being a peaceful environment.

Antong actually shared his journey in his memoir *A Redemptive Path Forward*. His experiences and mentorship skills have an impact on the way I mentor today. I learned from Antong how to build relationships and reduce violence. We share many similarities in that we are both what I refer to as human antibodies. We go in and strengthen communities using existing resources. We also have the ability to build relationships faster than any mentor, counselor, or youth worker because we earn the trust and the confidence of the young people we seek to serve. We are both relatable due to the fact that we have been through what the young people have gone through. I've used this approach throughout my whole career.

Andre Robinson out of Milwaukee is another example of a leader I admire. Based in Wisconsin, his story was similar to Antong's. He went to prison, got out, and to this day has been doing work in Milwaukee public schools reducing violence and recruiting other leaders to do the same.

In Baltimore, I met Billy Stanfield, a kingpin who went to prison. When he got out, he started The Impact Church. The Impact Church became known for working in schools like Fredrick Douglas, known for its challenges. The school was featured on HBO for its level of violence. He went in with other former gang members like himself who have changed their lives and now work with the youth to keep them out of gangs and away from violence.

The Feurtado brothers were the biggest drug kingpins in Queens, New York. They had one of the largest gangs in NYC, the 7 Crowns. The gang had over 1,500 members back in the day. Both went in for big sentences. Their story is well documented. Today, these guys are out and doing tons of poignant work in Queens.

Torrey Barrett was out of Chicago. His father has a church on the southside, and they started the KLEO Community Center. It stands for Keep Loving Each Other. He named it after his sister who was killed in a domestic violence incident. Torrey has a similar story to many of the other changemakers I've worked with, but they were part of a church, and that was my first time experiencing a church that was really leaning into the black community. Torrey's church and his father, the senior pastor, reflect the impact of churches in their communities.

Bob's approach was that these grassroots leaders should be the solution. He introduced me to all these leaders who most people don't know about because they operated underneath the radar. It was these changemakers, however, that created an impact in those communities. It shouldn't be the big organizations that get all the money. It should be leaders that know the community, are from the community, are closest to the problem, have hands-on experience with the problem, and have figured out how to achieve against the odds. Those are the real change agents. True change matters most on the ground, with the people.

AFFLICTION

During this time, Tanya and I were still together and attempting to maintain a long-distance relationship. She had some time left at Hampton. She was studying speech pathology, so she was taking the time to prepare for the prospect of a new career upon graduation. A future together might have been possible if things had gone well, but fate had other plans.

The distance proved to be more challenging than we believed it would be. Finally, everything came to a head one night in DC. Her parents were staying in their summer house, and she came back into town to stay at her parents' empty Maryland home.

Although I had been there earlier in the day, we were supposed to hang out later that night in DC. In accordance with our plans, I met my friend downtown for a couple of drinks. It was getting late, and she never called for us to come and meet up with her and her friends. I was upset, and I called her, but she did not answer. Eventually, I decided to go by the house to make sure she was alright.

When I pulled up to the house, I saw a car that I did not recognize in the driveway with a Hampton tag. My mind started swirling; *what is this all about?* It was about one in the morning, so I knocked on the door. I know she's there because I can see her car parked out front. Instantly, I start thinking, *what the hell is going on?* I'm asking myself, *Kwame, what are you about to do in this scenario right now?* I was inebriated, upset, and could feel what was going on. My emotions were mounting.

By now, I've known Bob and the Woodson family for so long that I had keys to the house and codes to the alarm. I was so close to being family to the point where I could go over to the house by myself and hang out. I went up to the garage and opened it with the code, which I shouldn't have done. My friend was still in the car and had no idea what was going on as I went into the house. I walked into the foyer, and I could hear the dog barking in its cage. I repeated to myself, *remain calm.*

Tanya came downstairs and told me that I needed to leave. In the heat of the moment, I pulled out my phone and threatened to call her father and let him know what's going on. But, I did not want to be misinterpreted. Come to find out, someone upstairs, hiding in the closet, had called the police. My friend came inside, urging me to leave. I followed him back out and called Bob. I told him what was going on, that I didn't want any problems and I was leaving. By the time I exited the garage, seven cops had pulled up and posted up at their cars with infrared beams pointed at us.

One beam was in the center of my forehead, and another two were pointed at my chest. They closed in on us, and I just put the phone down on the car in the garage and made sure I didn't cause a scene. Bob could still hear what was going on through the phone. The cops put us both in handcuffs. They sat me on the front steps and put my friend in the back of a squad car.

God was on my side with how that situation played out. They asked me what had happened, and I told them the whole story. I told them I was drunk, that I had been to jail before, and that I had not done anything wrong. I just shouldn't have gone inside. When my gut told me what I knew was happening, I should've turned around and left. The officer let my friend out of the car, removed the handcuffs, and told us to get home safe and get out of there. They let me drive home drunk in Silver Springs, Maryland.

This became a big dilemma in my relationship with Bob. I was about three or four years into my time at CNE, working for Bob. I remember the embarrassment of having to go into the office the next day. So much of it was a blur, looking back at it now. I went into the office to talk to Terence about what I should do next. By this time, Terence was my day-to-day mentor, my boss, and my really close friend. Bob was removed from the daily work and more in the limelight, drawing attention to the cause and working with the big names in Washington. Terence became an immediate mentor to me during that time. He was always the middleman between Bob and me as the number two in the office. He told me that I needed to talk to Bob and get right with him about the whole situation.

Bob returned from their summer house the day after the incident. I went to talk to him about what happened and apologize for my part in it. I thought he was going to fire me. I thought that would be the end of the whole experience and the work I was doing. I told him that I didn't go in there to hurt anybody. I was just trying to figure out what was going on. I didn't want the cops or anyone else involved, but the situation got out of hand in no time.

Bob told me that he understood. He mainly was upset about the police coming to his neighborhood but understood where I was coming from. He knew both his daughter and I were wrong in our own ways. But, even though he understood, things weren't ever going to be the same.

I kept working at CNE. This was the last straw for Tanya and me, and we stopped talking. The period after that was difficult. I not only broke up with Tanya, but I also broke up with the whole family. I was tight with her mom, brothers, nephews, nieces, and all of that had to stop since we were no longer in that kind of relationship. I still worked with Bob, but we were never as close as we were before.

Over time, Bob and I developed more of a professional relationship. I think if you asked him, he would probably say he had a better relationship with me after the breakup because Tanya was his baby. For him, it was likely a relief. He and I could now just be friends and be boys and go to the bar and drink and travel together versus me being his daughter's boyfriend. We moved forward, and continued to do good work and travel around the country, making a difference.

Although I never admitted this, the breakup was the beginning of a dark period for me. I fell into a pit of depression. I was heartbroken. I had been cheated on twice, and it hit me just as hard, except I wasn't as angry this time. I was just devastated. I started hanging out in town, spending money on frivolous things to fill the void.

My valley moment was when I got a call from the apartment complex telling me that all of my stuff was outside and I needed to come and get it. I had fallen too far behind on the rent. This was my first time experiencing homelessness. I told my parents and my boss that the water main broke at my apartment. I was so embarrassed and so mortified that I couldn't bring myself to tell them what was actually going on.

A lady that worked in the rental office actually stood outside and watched over my stuff until I could get there. When I arrived, she instructed me to go get a rental truck and that she would watch my belongings until I returned. Again that was God looking out for me. She did not have to do that for me, but she did. That small act of kindness at that moment meant so much to me.

I went to the closest Uhaul to get a truck, and there were some workers out front hanging around looking for something to do. A black guy named Tony who helped people do different projects was there, so I offered him what little money I could, and he came with me. Tony helped me load up all of my stuff and put it in storage.

At this point, I had messed up my credit, and money wasn't right because I didn't make good decisions with it. I lived out of my car for a few months while I figured myself out. I kept my clothes and my suits in the trunk. I slept in my car on some nights and others in the office. I most often showered at the gym. Nobody knew about it. My mother didn't know Terence, Bob, none of them. I learned that sometimes the only way out is through. I was forced to feel the pain of the breakup and take ownership of the poor decisions I made that landed me without a place to live.

I've had multiple falls and trials throughout my life. The breakup and the hard times I experienced in DC had only been part of it, but I've always found a way to get back up no matter what I faced. Part of that desire to keep going and motivation comes from being encouraged and helped by mentors. My mentors came in various forms, including formal mentors or people lending their time for a moment, a season, and some for a lifetime. They all made a difference in my life or from whom I've learned from.

The Violence Free Zone had a major impact on me. Coming out of jail and coming up to DC, I thought I was the only one who had that kind of experience. I never met anybody at Hampton like myself or with my background. You just didn't hear about people like me being considered useful to society, and for this reason, I thought I was alone. Bob, Terence, and the CNE showed me that there were many people like me with similar backgrounds who used their experiences and setbacks to help other people.

The hard times I faced in DC became one of the lowest points in my life. I struggled deeply, but my mentors taught me that you need to take your worst moments and transform them into success. I didn't know it at the time, but I was about to do just that.

To My Parents

I would like to thank you for putting everything on the line for me in challenging times. I was a young person, and I made terrible decisions. People automatically question your track record and credibility when your child gets into trouble. People somehow blame you for your child's decisions. My actions back then were not your fault; they were mine. Even though I decided to be a knucklehead, you never gave up on me. You supported me. You have always supported me. For your love, I am forever grateful.

PowerMyLearning Staff

Q Parker, Ardre, Kwame

Kwame Jr at Falcons Game

Kwame Johnson Action
Pic with Son

8: Transform

Always believe that the best is yet to come.

|KJ|

Angel of Mine

It is often said *that the sun will come out tomorrow.* After struggling with money, homelessness, and heartbreak, I worked hard to feel and be better. For me, tomorrow meant a year later, and the sun would be my future wife, Sabria.

Sabria was born and raised outside of Richmond, Virginia. She majored in nursing during college, starting at Virginia Commonwealth University. She had a passion for getting into a good nursing program, so she ended up going to Hampton University like her mother. We were at Hampton at the same time, but she was a year older than me, so we were in different crowds. We ran into each other in the yard once or twice, so we were a familiar face to one another but didn't know each other formally.

On a rainy night in DC, I was hanging out at Ozios on 18th and M St NW, where I always went to relax after work. I saw Sabria hanging with her friends. She looked familiar to me. I didn't know her name, but we caught eyes a few times while we were there.

I was actually talking to another young lady while I was there and went to the restroom. When I walked by Sabria, we both sort of stopped each other and said, "Did you go to Hampton?" I never made it to the bathroom or back to talk to that other girl. It was honestly fate that Sabria and I crossed paths that night. Later I learned that she was never really planning on going for a drink. Instead, she had been convinced by some friends to hang out. She was just visiting DC and had moved to Houston after graduating from Hampton. When we met, Sabria was a contract nurse and was just passing through.

From that night forward, Sabria and I began a courtship. We started talking on the phone and connecting with one another. But, more importantly, we were building a friendship. When we started going out, she helped me heal. Over time, she helped me create a home in a city where I felt alone. Her next contract was in New York City, and she traveled back and forth to DC every weekend to see me. The long-distance thing got old a year into the contract, so she took a new contract at John

Hopkins University in Baltimore, Maryland. She lived in Columbia, and I lived in Silver Springs.

We continued to date and got closer and closer to each other, spending more time together making our relationship official. A year later, we moved in together. She continued to motivate me and push me in my career from that point forward.

She'd tell me, "Kwame, you've been here for six years. Is Bob going to have a succession plan for you? What's next?"

Sabria encouraged me to see that I could do anything. She helped me realize that I learned a lot from Bob and Terence, and I could be just as great as they are. I could be a vice president. I could be a CEO. She motivated me to start looking at some other opportunities. I felt dedicated to Bob and Terence for giving me a chance from when I was in college when I made mistakes, and it was hard for me to say that it was probably time for me to move on. They had given and taught me so much. Terence especially had taught me how to tie a tie and how to be a young professional in DC.

I remember meeting with Terence, and he told me, "Kwame, Bob's not leaving. I'm here, and you've got a lot of talent." He encouraged me to quietly look at some other opportunities. He even served as a reference. Sabria continued to push me and motivate me, which she's done throughout my whole career. She's inspired me to take on new opportunities and new challenges. I realize today that a man needs a strong woman to help him realize a greater vision. Although I've always had vision I have not always had the discipline and the confidence to take the next step. Sabria gave me all these attributes and more.

After seven years of working with Bob, I realized that Bob was a giant in the community, a giant in the country. He spoke on Fox and at media outlets throughout the country and took meetings with presidents. He was a giant, and rightfully so. He had done the work to walk as a giant. I also recognized that giants cast big shadows. I was either going to remain stuck in Bob's shadow or begin a path all my own. It wasn't easy, but I eventually left Bob and Terence at CNE. I had to let all my different leaders around the country know, and I had to let Bob know.

I told Bob and Terence, "You all have taken me so far. I want to get to what you have. I want to get to the next level of my career. I'm young, and I've got a lot of ambition, a lot of talent. I want to reach my full potential." Terence was very supportive, but Bob was a little upset about it in his own way. Unfortunately, Bob didn't take it too well. We didn't talk for a very long time when I first left. Over the years, we've gotten to a better place.

I was gearing up for two new roles. One as a new staff member at the Communities and Schools National Office. And the second as Sabria's husband. We'd been together for four years. She knew that a proposal was coming because we had discussed it on several occasions.

When I knew we were serious, I talked to her parents about getting married. We had also been living together for close to two years, and it was on our minds. I decided that I was going to do it on Christmas. I wanted to make it a little funny. I sometimes have a weird sense of humor. I went out to try and find the funniest Christmas gift I could. This was going to be one last test to see how she received the gift. I thought, *what can I get her that would be a funny but also a nice gift?* So I went out and found those one-piece pajamas that you had as a kid, and I wrapped it up in a nice box with shiny holiday gift wrap.

She played it off really well, like she was happy with the gift, appreciated it, this and that. When she turned around, I had the ring out, down on one knee, and I proposed. It was a pretty special moment. Sabria cried, and I was so grateful for her being a part of my life and helping me work toward who I was really meant to be.

We decided upon a destination wedding because we both have tons of family, and we didn't want to break the bank by trying to host the wedding in DC. We realized that if we made it a destination wedding, the people that really wanted to be there and had the means to come would make it happen.

We selected a resort in Punta Cana. An all-inclusive, all-you-can-eat stay for five days and four nights around $500 per person, flight included. That's all you had to pay, $500 for your flight and hotel. We got a really great deal, and fifty people ended up coming to the wedding.

All my friends from high school that I continue to stay in touch with, family and friends, it was a really great time. Each day we did something different. One day we had a pool party, other days, we did the excursions at the resort, and we had dinner as a family every night.

The wedding on the beach is what Sabria requested. Since she was a little girl, it had been her dream to get married on the beach. My older brother, a pastor in Michigan, was the officiant. His presence made the exchange of our vows sweet and personal. We were married under a gazebo on the beach. It was a dream come true. I was marrying my best friend, and my whole family was there supporting me the way they had supported me through all the moments of my life. On that day, I recognized that everything I had gone through was to get to the best gift of my life: My wife.

After we were married, we lived in a townhouse in Woodbridge, Virginia, making a home and a life together. Then, on February 7th, 2013, God saw fit to bless our union with a child. The birth of Kwame Jr. was the most precious extension of the love Sabria and I shared. I was proud of him the moment he arrived. After that, my goal became to be his mentor, his safe space, and the best dad possible.

When Kwame Jr. was born, my parents had just moved to Virginia, and they were about twenty miles south of us. Ever since I left Syracuse and went to college, I tried to convince my parents to move out of Syracuse. All the kids were now gone from home. There were no opportunities in Syracuse, and it was very cold. There was just no reason for them to stay. When Kwame Jr was born, that was the final piece for them. That was finally enough for them to leave Syracuse after being there for forty years. They sold their house and made some money. They had a couple of properties there at the time. They could finally enjoy retirement. After thirty years in the school system, my father retired, and my mom was already retired. It was perfect. We had the grandparents there and the grandchild.

After the first year of our marriage, Sabria and I realized it was time for us to take our next step together and get some more space. We were renting and decided to buy a piece of property and build our house from the ground up. That was a big milestone for us as first-time homebuyers in our early thirties. It was an amazing experience to learn about the construction process and have a hands-on say in how our home would look when it was finished. We were building more than a house. We were building a home in one another's hearts.

WHEN PURPOSE CALLS

My work at Communities and Schools National Office was laser-focused on dropout prevention. As the nation's largest dropout prevention organization, we wanted to do everything possible to help kids stay in school. This battle had personal meaning to me after all I experienced in my personal life. The goal was to surround students with a community of support, empowering them to stay in school and achieve in life.

When I worked for Bob at CNE, I was a Program Director. There was little fundraising involved but not directly. My role was mainly to lead the programs we had across the country. I knew I needed to get some fundraising experience to become the CEO I wanted to be. Whether you're for-profit or nonprofit, all CEOs have to be able to go out and raise money for their organizations.

A Director of Corporate Relations role opened up at Communities and Schools, and I decided to go for it. I guess you could call it, *fake it till you make it* since I'd never done corporate fundraising, but I knew this was my next big step in my career, and I went all in.

Working for a large nonprofit gave me tremendous insight. They were well-funded, and I learned from those leaders how to fundraise for my organization and build relationships with corporate giants. Before they gave me that shot, I was not a fundraiser, but learning and developing that skill helped me become the CEO I am today.

As the Director of Corporate Relations, I traveled across the nation, raising money in different cities to support our local affiliates. We had a chapter of Communities and Schools in every city, New York, Chicago, LA, and Atlanta. We'd raise money with some of the big names in corporate America, Coca-Cola, McDonald's, Taco Bell, Wells Fargo, Bank of America, and Walmart.

I excelled at Communities and Schools, further solidifying my passion for youth development. Young people have a lot of defining potential but can also be victims of their circumstances, so being able to mentor them and provide them with opportunities that they might not see for themselves became a driving force for me. I became so passionate about it, and the more work I did, the closer I became to the people we were helping. I wanted to get closer to the Anthony's and Shank's of the world, get into the local communities, and ensure impact in the trenches.

The job at Communities and Schools kept me on the road every other week, bouncing from city to city. It felt like I never got a chance to plant my feet. With Kwame Jr. at home and Sabria working pretty much every day as a nurse, finding a place to settle in and integrate with the local community was on my heart.

Now three years into the job— with my mother-in-law Adrian helping us out and watching Kwame Jr. at the house— I realized I wanted to lead a nonprofit that worked with kids every day in a local jurisdiction. Instead of traveling the country like I did working for Bob at CNE and at Communities and Schools, I wanted to get into the community at the closest level and impact the lives of young people all around me. Sabria and I started looking at all the different things you look for when raising a family and considering where to plant your roots. We pondered where would be a good city for family and friends, with good schools and job opportunities for both of us. Atlanta quickly rose to the top because it checked many boxes for us. I was familiar with Atlanta. During my travels, I had some high school friends in Atlanta; my younger brother was in Atlanta, the cost of living was reasonable, and it wasn't too far from either of our families. Atlanta was known as a black Mecca. After fifteen years in DC, we determined that it was time to make a new city and state home.

BECOMING

Before I became an Executive Director and later a CEO, I learned how to fulfill those roles by watching others in DC. So often, particularly for black people, there are roles we aspire to have, but we may not feel competent enough, or we may not have the resources to go after them. It takes a lot of work to get to the point where you can walk into a room and know that you have the skill set necessary to lead an organization.

There was never a time when I was not in observance of leaders like Bob and Terence. I watched the way they spoke to crowds and on TV. They always demonstrated confidence in their ability to communicate their work.

Andre Robinson told me something I've never forgotten. "Communication is very important because when you open your mouth, you tell the world who you are."

I started out by trying to mimic what they did, and in the process of mimicking, I picked up my own approach and my own style of communicating. As a black male, especially a black male with a background, I felt I had to communicate more effectively and articulately.

Being a listener and an observer of leaders is a huge part of the learning process. Too often, I see young leaders who think they have all the answers. Listening is far more important. When you recognize that there is value in becoming a sponge, you will learn something valuable every time. You don't always have to be the one talking. Watching others do what you're trying to do is also key. I also learned the importance of your reputation and its fragility. Reputation is so pivotal for becoming a leader and maintaining that leadership. The reputation of the listener and of the learner builds your credibility. I began to ask myself how I could take what other well-respected leaders in the community or in the country were doing and apply that to myself. Carefully crafting the pieces of how successful leaders acted and presented themselves and formed the solid foundation for the exercise of my own style of leadership.

When I worked on 16th and K St., blocks from the White House, I was right inside the city. I would see these different businessmen and leaders, how they would dress and carry themselves at all times of the day. When I went to lunch, everyone was suited. When I went to happy hour, everyone had on suits and ties. I went from getting my shoes at Payless and my clothes at Walmart to buying tailored suits and knowledge of various ways to tie a tie. I learned how to dress for the occasion, how to coordinate a suit, and always be on point regardless of what meeting or environment I was in. Perception is reality, and you get one chance to make a first impression in the business world. That impression you make is invaluable when it comes to your reputation, how people perceive you, and ultimately how they treat you.

All of these little pieces, these nuances of leadership I learned particularly in DC. They seem like simple things on the surface, but when you put them together, all the relationships, the confidence, appearance, and how you speak, all of those pieces together make a CEO. If you don't have all the pieces in place, you won't be the leader or CEO that you want to be. I learned these things by being a sponge, watching and learning from my various teachers and mentors. Emulating their communication and leadership styles in my own way, putting my own spin on them to stay true to who I am. After years in DC, navigating the corporate world, I was ready to step into my first CEO role and become what I'd been working towards, what I'd been preparing for all this time.

I was finally ready to step into the CEO position I'd been grooming myself for my entire career. My search for a position as a CEO led me to an Executive Director role at PowerMyLearning, a youth development organization, and I went after it.

Mentee Anthony and Kwame Jr

Day One Friends

News Interview with Karyn Greer

Arthur and Angie Blank

Sabria, Kwame, and Chris Tucker

9: GROW

We must vow to change what we are if
we dare to become what we might be.

|KJ|

85 SOUTH

Just over a year after building our first home in DC, we made the bold decision to relocate to Atlanta. Kwame Jr. was still young, just turning two years old. Sabria supported me as she's done my entire career. We were moving to a whole new city where we didn't know a ton of people, and I would have to start from scratch after building my career in DC.

Sabria—a nurse by trade—immediately got a job at a children's hospital in Atlanta. I secured a position at PowerMyLearning. When I came to DC, I thought— growing up in the north— that this was living in the south. Atlanta is the real south, and I soon learned the meaning behind the phrase southern hospitality.

It's kind of like when you get off the plane to Miami, and that humidity just hits you in the face, you instantly know that you are somewhere different. The entire Atlanta community welcomed us with open arms, unlike anything I had experienced before.

DC was great when I was a young professional, grinding and growing my career, but I learned that DC was not as much of a collaborative city as Atlanta is. The community was not as supportive, especially for blacks. Atlanta has a base of black leaders who encourage one another and support each other. That level of black excellence existed in DC to an extent but not in the same sense as Atlanta. DC was such a transient city, so big and diverse that you could never build a community the way you can in Atlanta.

Coming to Atlanta, if I wanted to sit down and meet with someone, they would agree to meet with me within two weeks. In DC, it would take a couple of months to schedule if they would even sit down with you. They may do a phone call a few months down the line, but they're not going to sit down to dinner with you.

But *that* is the Atlanta way. Experiencing professionalism and hospitality in this realm enabled me to ignite my career, leapfrog, and accomplish much more. Atlanta accepted my family and me immediately and became a place we could really call home.

POWERMYLEARNING

At the age of thirty-two, I landed the role of Executive Director at PowerMyLearning. I saw it as an opportunity to become a CEO, particularly in the youth development space, which was my goal all along. The staff had worked with their former leader for ten years before her retirement, and they welcomed me with open arms.

They were doing great work in schools helping kids get caught up in learning. They provided a number of different tools, resources, and technology and really bridged the learning gap through digital learning. Too often, the kids in the schools we support don't have proper internet at home. They don't have access to technology and the learning equipment, resources, games, and digital learning platforms that middle-class and wealthy families have. At PowerMyLearning our goal was to go into those schools and provide those resources. We would take laptops from companies or individuals, refurbish them, turn them into learning machines, and put software on them. Then, we'd go in and train the family on how to use that device for in-home learning. Assistance with digital learning is more important now than ever. The need to learn digitally is increasing. When I first started working for PowerMyLearning, one out of four families didn't have those resources available in Atlanta. So we went up to schools and helped bring digital learning closer to kids and families in need.

When I came into the organization, it had been around for ten years but was still in startup mode. They had a small budget of about $500,000. My goal was to take all of the experience that I acquired in DC, my fundraising experience, and experience traveling around the country and use that to help this organization go to the next level.

In the nonprofit sector, organizations are structured similar to corporations, so this role at PowerMyLearning was based out of New York, 501(c)(3) status, but they have offices in Atlanta. I came in as the Executive Director of the Atlanta office, but I was reporting to the New York headquarters. PowerMyLearning was different, which shed light on the different structures that exist in the nonprofit world. By taking these different roles and working in the nonprofit space for so long, I positioned myself to finally be ready for the mantle of CEO.

PowerMyLearning was the best-kept secret in Atlanta and my first shot at being the head guy of a larger organization. I leaned into the role, using my experience from DC, and took the Atlanta sector of the organization to the next level. We started with building up the brand, ensuring everyone in the city knew who we were, what we did, and why the work was so important to the community. Next, I utilized my fundraising experience and started meeting with funders all over the city.

Atlanta being such a welcoming city, working with other leaders and business people was a terrific experience. When I reached out to a funder or a corporation, they were prompt and supportive. People would say, "Hey, let's grab lunch in a couple of weeks," and they'd sit down with me and connect. I filled my calendar with meetings. Some weeks I was doing upwards of forty meetings. I've always had a high volume pace in cultivating relationships and meeting new people. Whether it be a corporate funder, a foundational partner, individuals, the community, or another CEO, I met with as many people as I could, building and exploring those relationships and chances for partnership.

Over a period of three years, PowerMyLearning in Atlanta tripled its revenue and doubled the number of kids in the community we were serving. The organization completely transformed. We went from being the best-kept secret in Atlanta to a well-known brand. Our exposure and funding grew. We brought on more staff, and I could see the fruits of everything I learned in DC applied in real-time to the community in Atlanta.

I built a reputation as a leader in Atlanta, networking and meeting the right people. Through that, I got a lot of different awards, Forty Under Forty, accolades, and recognition for all the things my team was able to accomplish.

During my three years at PowerMyLearning, I was able to take on the mantle of mentorship. I groomed my replacement Richard Hicks, now the CEO of the organization. Richard had been there since the beginning when I arrived, but he'd never gotten a shot to be the CEO or the leader we both knew he could be. A Georgia country boy born and bred, he was dedicated and passionate about helping young people. So I poured into him all I knew at the time, even though I was still a young leader growing in my career and Richard was older than me.

When we met, Richard didn't have the right level of confidence in his career, which is a major roadblock most leaders, especially black leaders, face. They have the skills they've worked hard to develop over their careers, but they don't have the confidence to lean into it. They don't believe in themselves, which ties into not being comfortable enough to tell their story. Young leaders don't learn a lot of skills while in college, including how to be confident and recognize the power in their stories and embrace the skills they've worked to accumulate.

I gave Richard all of my pieces, everything I'd learned from DC, Bob, and Terence. I shared with him how to communicate, how to meet with people and fundraise, how to dress and build his reputation. Richard really leaned into the power in his story. He embraced the mantle of CEO as the leader he always aspired to be. He was given a chance to be Executive Director after I left PowerMyLearning, and continued growing and flourishing. Under his leadership, the Atlanta office of PowerMyLearning branched out and became its own nonprofit outside of the New York office. Now called InspiredU, Richard became the permanent CEO of the organization and continues to do amazing work that he's incredibly passionate about.

It wasn't until Richard really came into his own as the head of PowerMyLearning that I decided to leave. Being able to help him grow and realize his potential as a leader was such a rewarding experience in my career. I was able to pass the lessons and mentorship that I received to someone else just as it was done for me. Finally, after giving all my lessons to Richard, I was ready to move forward. It was finally my time to become the CEO.

EACH ONE, TEACH ONE.

After being at PowerMyLearning for three years, I got a call from an old friend, Carol Lewis, about an opportunity at Big Brothers, Big Sisters. Carol and I met when I worked for Communities In Schools. She was over the Georgia chapter of the organization. A CEO position had been made available, and she mentioned my name to the search firm, Boardwalk, which specializes in placing minority talent in nonprofit leadership roles.

After twenty-five years of leadership under the same CEO, who was preparing for retirement, Big Brothers Big Sisters was looking for a successor. They hired Boardwalk to find their next leader. Sam Pettway, the leader of Boardwalk, a great leader who became a great mentor of mine, reached out to me.

"We got your name from Carol Lewis," He said. "We'd like you to interview with us for the Chief Executive Officer position at Big Brothers Big Sisters."

I wasn't actively looking for a position like this, but I knew about the organization and their values really aligned with mine. Big Brothers Big Sisters is all about mentorship, which I believe is priority number one when working with youth in America. Mentoring has so many positive impacts and allows leaders and change-makers to work one on one with so many kids to push and inspire them to achieve in their lives. I wasn't ready, but I knew this was something I had to try. Although I hadn't studied or prepared, I wasn't sure I wanted to leave PowerMyLearning yet but, that's how God works.

The first thing I did was go home and talk to Sabria. Sabria's seen me through so many changes and big decisions in my life, always guiding me and encouraging me to see the value in my own skills and career. I knew I wanted to pursue this opportunity, but I couldn't do this without her by my side. She encouraged me to really think about what I wanted.

It was the next step in my career, a really big step. It put me back in the mentoring space which is my talent, my passion, and in a bigger more impactful role. I'd only been at PowerMyLearning for three years, and I questioned if I really wanted to leave so soon? These thoughts circled in my mind for a few days, but I decided to go in for the interview.

I only had a couple of days to prepare for the interview process. I spoke with Sam on Friday and interviewed on Monday. They had three or four final candidates to interview, and they fit me in at eight in the morning, which meant I had to go in first. The truth is, I had been preparing for this opportunity my entire career.

Any question they had about youth development, fundraising, and how to create change in troubled communities elicited a natural response from me. In the interview, I demonstrated my fundraising experience and my track record at PowerMyLearning over the last three years. As I was speaking, I was also proving to myself that I could actually do it. I had always watched others but never been in the driver's seat to put it to the test. My words took flight as I leaned into my youth development background and being a youth who benefited from programs like Big Brothers Big Sisters.

The interview with Boardwalk became an incredibly special and symbolic moment for me because it was the first time I shared my entire story with no holds barred. Of course, pieces of my story were on the internet, but something in that interview clicked for me. It was, in fact, the moment I became comfortable in my own skin. I witnessed my story become my superpower.

David Clark, the board chair of Big Brothers Big Sisters at the time, asked me the last question in the interview.

"What did you do to prepare for this interview today?"

"I've been preparing for this my whole life," I answered.

The interview went incredibly well, and I left with a renewed sense of purpose and solidarity in my heart. The next day a member from the interview committee reached out and said, "We like you and want you to be the new CEO at Big Brothers Big Sisters."

They offered to take me to the office and show me around to introduce me to the leadership team. The team consisted of six members including, The Director of Human Resources, the Vice President of Programs, a Chief Financial Officer, Chief External Relationship Manager, and an executive assistant. I often found myself being the youngest person in the room, and I drew on that confidence I'd been cultivating over the years. To be thirty-five, coming in to lead a team of people all older than me who had all been there longer than I had was a task I did not take lightly.

Not only did I not have a ton of experience as a CEO, but I also did not arrive with a leadership team, fundraising team, or my own executive assistant. These pieces were new opportunities that I had to get comfortable with and lean into. I had to position my mind to be ready for the opportunity.

Later, I learned from Dave after I was hired that the search committee told the board they found their person, even before interviewing the other candidates. God placed this opportunity before me at the right time, and I now know that it was all a part of my journey.

Coming from the east side of Syracuse, and Jamesville, to now being down on 17th and Peachtree St in this big building as the CEO of an organization with tremendous reach was food for my soul. The war wounds I sustained over the years only made me stronger. In full transparency, there was a voice inside my head that made me feel like there was a possibility I was not prepared enough. There was another level of confidence I had to go out and get.

Truth be told, I was intimidated by the role, even though it was granted to me and that I had worked to earn it. I was replacing someone who had been there for twenty-five years and was much older than me. I was also taking the helm of an organization for the first time with a team of fifty people and a four million dollar budget to boot. Moreover, I had my own board to report to.

Looking back, I can see that I had previously done this work in different shapes and forms since my first job at the Center for Neighborhood Enterprises. I had seen this work being done at a high level, and now it was my time to execute and put my own touch on it. I had to push through that little voice in my head that was, in fact, a naysayer and go after it.

BBBS Board Chairs- Peter
Lauer and Dave Clark

BBBS Featured at DragonCon

Rugged Maniac Race with fellas

Mrs. Nunn

BBBS Ribbon Cutting Grand Opening Ceremony

To Sabria and Kwame Jr.

Sabria

You were the sole driving force behind my first step and leap of faith in my professional career. What I didn't know was that I had to leave the Woodson Center after seven years of service and pursue a new role that would expand my capacity and allow me to reach my full potential in order for my dream to manifest before my eyes. Without you, I would have stayed and never left. I'm a CEO today because of your faith in me.

Building a legacy with you means we are doing something that our families have not done. We have achieved beyond the hopes and dreams of many people and their wishes for us. We are showing our families what is possible when you bring two dynamic leaders together. Not only does our family win, but our entire tribe wins.

Kwame Jr.

I never want you to take what we have created for you for granted. Strive hard at all times. Even though you have been fortunate to have a lot of things given to you through our achievements, never cease to create your own. Your mom and I are both in the giving business. Remember us as givers to our community. Know that a difference is all we have ever strived to make. I hope that this same spirit of giving will be abundant in your soul. Always strive to help other people in some type of way.

10: EVOLVE

One day when it is all said and done, we will recognize that it is not the strong who survive; instead, it is those who evolve.

|KJ|

DAY ONE. ONE DAY.

On my first day at Big Brothers Big Sisters, I had to address fifty people that I didn't know as their new CEO. They also did not know me. Significant leadership changes can sometimes cause tension on both sides. Instead of laying out some big vision for the organization initially, I planned on going in with a willingness to listen and share openly about my story and my journey. We needed time to figure out where we were going and how we were going to get there. It was vital for me to lean into relationship building and mesh with my new team on that first day. I have always built solid relationships by leaning in and sharing details about who I am and telling my story. Today, I continue to do that as part of my strategy as a leader.

I met with the leadership team first. I began by saying, "None of us know each other, so let's get comfortable with each other. I'm not coming in with my own team. I want to get to know all of you and work with you. If it's a good fit for both sides, we'll continue." That was my message to them, and I'm happy to share that I still have the same leadership team outside of one person years later. I hear a lot about leaders who come into an organization, dismiss the current team and begin with their own teams. Yet, some leaders rely upon what they've done in the past and mold the new organization to fit a prior vision. I came in and worked with who was there, and we grew together. I wanted to use people who had already been there and were dedicated.

In some cases, individuals held eighteen years of dedication to the organization. I wanted to help them win and win alongside them. Not with new people or by myself. I spent my first few weeks as CEO analyzing the organization. What were we doing wrong? What do we need to change to do better and in what ways do we need to grow? I took it day by day, identified some key areas that we needed to focus on, and came back with my big three: finances, morale, and brand.

Priority one was financial. The organization had a lot of debt built up from bad decision-making in the past. We had a 30,000 square foot building in the middle of Midtown, a bustling area of downtown Atlanta, and many people thought we shouldn't be there. The organization experienced some growth from being located in Midtown, but our work happens in the community. When you become a Big Brother or Big Sister, you mentor someone in the community, at the park, going to the store, or the movies. All the different things that we adults do, we expect to bring your little brother or sister along with you, and experience life with them. That did not happen in our building, so I didn't see the need for the 30,000 square foot building in Midtown. We host events and programs in our building for our Littles but not enough to justify such a big building. I knew that to get us out of debt, we could sell our building, downsize to something more appropriate and get back into the communities we serve. It took three years and many ups and downs amidst the pandemic to finally get the deal done.

When I took over, there were some morale issues that required attention. We had a high turnover rate which adversely affects an organization's stability. The solution was a pretty basic thing for me. I knew how to build relationships and how to talk to people. I walked the floor every day and ran a weekly huddle where we got together as a team and shared updates and successes. I created a comment box for individuals to privately ask questions that they did not want to bring up in person or in front of everyone else on the team. During our staff meetings, I would address those questions and provide feedback which helped boost the morale of the team. I ran a salary analysis to see how competitive we were against others. The goal was to pay our people better and help make them happier in their work. We did a number of different initiatives to build morale and tackle the turnover rate.

Big Brothers Big Sisters was in Atlanta for over fifty years at this time, but they were no different than PowerMyLearning. They were also a best-kept secret because the brand went silent. So bringing more awareness to what we were doing was critical. We had a great mission, providing one-to-one mentors to thousands of kids across all twelve counties in the Atlanta area. The power of mentorship can change lives forever, so we needed to get out there and let the community know about our work and that we existed.

I have always made my brand the organization's brand. I tell people all the time, I'm the mascot, janitor, and sometimes the CEO of Big Brothers Big Sisters. I wore our swag everywhere I went, making connections and meeting with people. At every event, networking party, and table, I talked about the work to make sure everybody knew what Big Brothers Big Sisters was doing. We amped up our social media strategy, boosting our posts, website strategy, and telling our story on different social platforms. In partnership with our national office, we rebranded the Atlanta chapter. We changed our logo and colors, updated our website, and went for a bold approach to target a younger generation of potential mentors.

Big Brothers Big Sister started in New York in 1904, which meant we were around for over a hundred years. We were aware that, as an organization in Atlanta—but also as a network across the country—if you were over forty years old, you probably knew about Big Brothers Big Sisters. You likely grew up with us. We had commercials in the '80s and '90s. But all that stopped. The millennials and younger generations did not know about us. We knew we had to go after them and let them know that they could be a part of Big Brothers Big Sisters and that they could be mentors. We knew that a lot of them had already gone through the program; they just didn't have any affiliation with us as an adult living in Atlanta. So we began targeting them on social media, hosting luncheons with potential mentors and their companies at Coca-Cola, Home Depot, UPS, and several other corporations. We hosted happy hours and events that immersed us in the communities. I engaged in speaking conferences, whether at the Rotary or the westside of Atlanta at a communion meeting, the Buckhead Club, or the Gathering Spot. I was out there speaking about the work. My story, combined with the Big Brothers Big Sisters story, created a powerful energy source for the community to gravitate to.

When I joined, Peter Lauer, who was the board chair, had stepped in to be the CEO after the previous CEO retired. While they were searching, Peter worked as the interim CEO and did many things that helped ease the transition for me. One of our most significant initiatives was our recruiting partnership with Mayor Keisha Lance Bottoms. When I started, we had 1000 kids on our waiting list. These are kids who came in with their parents who said, "Hey, my child wants a mentor."

For me, that meant that it was our responsibility to find them one. There were a thousand of them, and some of them had been waiting for two years in communities like College Park and the westside of Atlanta. It was a big challenge initially, but I knew we had to get these students matched with mentors. We worked on that waiting list tirelessly and whittled it down to 500. I knew we needed a big partner, a prominent voice, to talk about the work and get the message out. The Mayor was one of the biggest names we were able to secure. I met with the Mayor's office and told her that we had about 500 kids on the waiting list needing mentors.

"How many kids are waiting for mentors in the city of Atlanta?" The Mayor asked.

I replied, "About a hundred."

At the time, most of the kids on the waiting list were boys, and that was always a challenge bringing more men in to become mentors. Together, we set a '100 Men to Mentor' challenge, and she made the push. We held five informational sessions at different spots around the community, the Mayor's office, the Gathering Spot, the Rice Center, and a local church on Cascade. She did the commercials letting the community know about these events, and we led the sessions.

There are times when society would have us believe that men of color, black men, in particular, aren't going to step up and be a part of something. There is a false narrative that we are disconnected from the community and not active in our homes. On the contrary, we had over 100 men of color coming to these informational sessions. At the end of the campaign, we had 400 men from across Atlanta signing up to be Big Brothers. Not only was that a big boost for the brand, but we were able to expand and provide mentions to more boys throughout the area.

People started to talk about the organization in a big way, and it helped to make us a household name. We became a major player in the youth development space in Atlanta. We also became more innovative in the way we approached our community and grew our programs. While in the process of moving the headquarters deeper into the community, I wanted to do more work in schools in the preliminary. Going to where the kids are, to the watering holes of America, is something I believe we need to do more of as a society. Too often, nonprofits say *come to me*, but my approach is that we must *go to them*. We must meet the kids where they are for maximum impact. Therefore, we started to grow site-based programs to go into schools and mentor the kids right on campus. We went into schools like Thomasville Elementary on the east side of Atlanta.

If there was any school from which a child could visualize failure, it would be Thomasville Elementary School. Thomasville is where acclaimed rapper and Atlanta native 2 Chainz went to school, right across from the Thomasville projects. Going to Thomasville, you get off I-20 to get to the east side, and on the way there, you pass a federal penitentiary a block from the school. You pass a landfill and juvenile facilities all a stone's throw away from these kids going to school every day.

I went there and met with Mr. Miles, the outstanding principal at Thomasville, and told him that we wanted to bring mentors into his school for some of the kids that are in high need. He told me about all the challenges facing these young people and Thomasville. For example, during lunchtime and specific school periods, the guards at the prison up the street would host gun practice and interrupt the school day with the sounds of gunfire. These were just some of the factors at play for the faculty and students at Thomasville. As a result, we implemented a program at Thomasville Elementary providing mentors to many students, and have been for the past few years.

Typically in our community-based program, you have to come down to Midtown and sign your children up, but when we go into a school, we have direct access to young people, guidance counselors, and other professionals that are more aware of the children's situations. We don't have to wait for parents to come down and see us. We can go in while the parents are at work, knowing their children will have a mentor and get that one-to-one experience during the school day in a safe and controlled environment.

We grew to a total of ten school partners across the metropolitan area. While our site-based programs grew, I knew that we also needed to give kids more exposure to career opportunities. Being in Atlanta, what I call *Corporate Candyland, I* saw it as an excellent opportunity to create a new program called Workplace Mentoring. A few communities across the country were doing something similar, but it had not been done in Atlanta.

I spoke to my brother Gayle Nelson, who ran the Miami office. He told me about this program they had with Carnival Cruise Line, which is run by an African American man. He told me that they had been working with them for a number of years. The kids would go to Carnival Cruise Line and be exposed to different business areas. They saw the marketing, finance, and sales departments and would also get matched with a mentor. The kids visited a couple of times a month while receiving a one-to-one mentorship experience paired with someone within the company. The initiative has since grown, and now hundreds of kids have matriculated through. After going through the program, some of these kids are actually now employed at Carnival Cruise Line.

I knew right away, that was something we needed to do in Atlanta; it only made sense. Atlanta has so many companies, and it would be an excellent opportunity to bridge the divide. We were fortunate in our partnership with one of the most well-known companies in Atlanta. Every month, kids travel to the Cox campus and get to experience corporate life. They see all the fantastic buildings, visit the food court, and learn about their work, which is an incredible experience for young people. There are mentors at Cox that keep in touch with some of the kids and open them up to all the different jobs and opportunities at places similar to Cox. Not just the big ones you hear about, but all the various departments and additional opportunities such as cybersecurity and things our students never hear about. In the program, the students receive exposure and a mentor that helps to guide them and show them how they were able to do it themselves. During this process, they are reminded that they have the power to do all things.

I believe young people have to see it to achieve it, especially young boys. It is life-altering to give them that exposure and the ability to see firsthand people who look like them in different environments. Through that access, you can show a kid who only knows one way of life, an entire world of possibility, and give them hope for their own future.

LEAN IN AND PIVOT

Unquestionable momentum and impact were being made at Big Brothers Big Sisters. We were thriving and meeting kids and their families right where they were to deliver services. And then, one day, everything changed in what felt like the blink of an eye. Not only was our city being shut down and programming suspended until further notice, but so was the whole world. By the time we were fully informed, we were at the heart of a global pandemic with the onset of the Covid-19 virus. How we lived, worked, learned, and socialized would be forever changed. As a result, our normal program delivery methods came to a screeching halt.

To make matters worse, the stress of what would become our new normal added tension to many households as families were forced to stay home and stay together. This also meant mounting frustrations for many and financial hardships. There were kids whose only meals were attained at school, let alone mentorship. How do you survive a scenario like this as a leader – a nonprofit leader– in that sort of climate? There was no playbook; no one knew what to do or what would happen next. We had to close our office down, and everyone had to work remotely. It was a huge lesson and a leadership journey for me as well. It was a week-by-week game plan. There weren't any year-long strategies that could be developed. The circumstances forced me to meet with my leadership team every day versus the once-a-week session we had previously. We began meeting every day for an hour to talk through issues. We discussed financials, staffing, and programming. We were able to pivot and take all of our programs to a virtual platform. The whole process of becoming a Big Brother or Sister and becoming a little brother or sister became virtual and was executed from any location. We never ceased to make matches and support mentorship.

We also shifted our team to provide more referral services. Families began to come to us and stress their need for food and other supplies. Housing, mental health services, and basic needs were already an issue before, but due to Covid, the impact was worse. As a mentoring organization, we could have placed services on a hiatus, but instead, we pivoted to meet the immediate needs of the families we served. In addition to making matches for mentorship, we connected families to food banks, housing and rental assistance programs, and mental health services. There was a noticeable surge of need for mental and emotional support as our world chartered foreign territory. We did not realize it at the time because we put our heads down and did the work, but we were fulfilling our original intent of transitioning more and more into the community despite the pandemic.

In addition to the impact on the service model and delivery methods for Big Brothers Big Sisters programming, the financial ramifications of the pandemic were significant. My goal was to secure funding for our staff to ensure ongoing programming. After close consultation with our CFO- Paul Shenk, and a great board member, Mark Titpon, who is over Iberia Bank in Georgia, we worked as a team to secure the first Paycheck Protection Program (PPP) loan in the state of Georgia. It was the first PPP loan issued to a nonprofit, corporation, and anyone during the pandemic. We secured the funding one week after the applications went live. I was determined for our organization to survive Covid.

We also transformed our events. Before the pandemic, we hosted five fundraising events per year, and we raised a great deal of funding. Our gala, golf tournament, and bowling events were staples in our fundraising plan. In light of new restrictions and mandates for capacity and events in general, it proved challenging to even consider hosting a gala with five hundred people— which we would have done at St. Regis. Instead, we opted to host it virtually. We also implemented a series of house parties with about twenty hosts around the city, each inviting ten to twenty people into their homes and broadcasting via the Livestream. Innovation also led to establishing a new event called the Iconic Mentor Auction that we hosted in January for National Mentor Month. We couldn't bring people into a bowling alley and bowl to benefit our work like in previous years; thus, the Iconic Mentor Auction was our answer. Leaders in the community and iconic figures like Shaq, Carol Tome the CEO of UPS, and Arthur Blank were a few heavy hitters who lent their support. We auctioned off a one-hour exclusive mentor-ship session with twenty different leaders and figures to benefit Big Brothers Big Sisters. People invested up to twenty thousand dollars for the opportunity of a life-time. Carol Tome was thrilled to be a part of helping our organization, and it was easy for her to sign up and do it. All she had to do was give an hour of her time to the highest bidder. Shaq gave an hour of his time as well. We raised over a hundred thousand dollars despite the new challenges we faced.

With a clear path to funding and continued effec-tiveness in our work and service to the community, our next order of business was orchestrating the sale of our headquarters in Midtown. The building went under contract just before the pandemic started. The pandemic was the worst possible thing for commercial real estate. We faced a delay, then another delay, and another. Most commercial real estate deals blew up during this time as developers and investors pulled back while the country was on lockdown. No deals were going on in the country, but we were extremely lucky.

We were working with an extended vision developer called Greystar, who wanted to build a large multi-family residence on our current site. They gave us the option to pull out and revisit the deal after everything passed, but we kept working together to keep the deal warm. Even though it tied up our property, they had access to it, and I knew that if we could keep the deal warm, it would eventually get done. We came together as a team, strategized, and finalized the sale.

We accomplished so many things that many nonprofits weren't able to do. Getting the first PPP loan, selling our building, taking the programs virtually, pivoting, and coming up with new events helped us get through this tumultuous time. We were able to close the year 2020 in the black when most nonprofits closed in the red. I couldn't have done it without the help of my amazing leadership team and board of directors. That year, in particular, reinforced the power of faith and teamwork. We must never forget that we have the power to triumph no matter the circumstance.

BBBS Board and Supporters

Legend Andrew Young

Receiving ATL Business
Chronicle 40 Under 40

Poker and Cigar Buddies

11: Ascend

To ascend is to bring forward the version of yourself that you were destined to become.

|KJ|

The Next Chapter

I t is without question that Covid was the onset of what would become our new normal. And while there are still many factors that we can not predict nor control, we are empowered to be more progressive in our thoughts. For Big Brothers Big Sisters, and for me, it simply means to push the needle to serve young people by any means necessary. My life is proof that if you are born in America, you have an opportunity. I don't care about the color of your skin. You have an opportunity.

While the fact that we each have an opportunity is not up for debate, I will always acknowledge that we are often placed further away from those opportunities, especially people of color. Plainly stated, we all have a chance, but not everyone has the same opportunity.

My goal as CEO is to focus our attention on going deeper into the communities with the highest need. We already serve ninety percent of our families in Atlanta, free and reduced lunch, low income, you name it, we will help to provide it. Yet there are still families that we are not reaching, but we will. Since relocating our headquarters, we are now positioned to set up satellite offices in different parts of the community. Atlanta continues to change in terms of gentrification. People are constantly in motion. Atlanta has the highest level of suburban poverty. As a nonprofit, I don't want to be tied to a building that might limit us long-term. Suppose at some point, the south westside is very different from today. In that case, I want to be able to move and have very flexible locations.

Instead of building in every part of the city or renting a space, my plan is to collaborate in various ways with other nonprofits, organizations, and schools. This will allow us to better serve families together. Whether that's a Boys and Girls Club or another youth development organization, as nonprofits, we serve families, so why not go into a space that's already in that community? Every decision that we make can be more intentional, and if the community changes and the need is no longer there, we will move our operations to where the need is. We will pivot like we've been doing for the last few years.

We're also going to be more intentional with serving families that are sometimes overlooked, like kids involved in the criminal justice system. Most nonprofits don't say it out loud, but their application process weeds out kids who have been in the criminal justice system. Kids like me. This is unfortunate as I am proof of the transformation that can happen as a result of access to mentorship. The seventeen-year-old version of me would not be eligible to enter into different programs because I have a criminal background. I want to see the scope of access granted for programming to a broader reach in an attempt to save more lives. There are scores of more young people who need our help. From the waterboys and foster care youth to the homeless youth, and LGBTQ youth, they all deserve what we can offer. Working to break down perceived barriers is also necessary. Sometimes people don't want to mentor youth who are different from them or have different orientations than what they're used to, but I want to remove those limiting beliefs. We're going to do a deeper dive into diverse populations. Hence positioning ourselves within the community will allow us to serve them better.

Another area of focus is Diversity, Equity, and Inclusion, or DEI. I wrote an op-ed that was picked up by the Atlanta Journal-Constitution after George Flyod's senseless murder titled "You Don't Have to Fear Me." I talked about my story, being a young man who made a lot of bad decisions, and the fact that I superseded my circumstances through mentorship. I highlighted the fact that the true heart for mentorship knows no color. One of my most prolific mentors was a white man, Steve Maynord, my high school track coach. He didn't fear me, he ran towards me and helped me.

Steve Maynord taught me that there are good white people who want to help you too, who don't care about your skin color and just want to see you succeed when everything is working against you. He helped so many young black boys go to college on sports scholarships. He was a cop, a hall monitor, a track coach, and a football coach. He worked in an urban school with primarily black kids and leaned in. He saw me as a human, and we need more of that.

You don't have to fear someone that doesn't look like you. A great deal of racism stems from fear. The work we're doing at Big Brothers Big Sisters brings different races together and becomes a part of that solution. We are matching hearts or services with hearts in need. I believe all different races together in a mentoring relationship enhances perspective and makes both sides better. We will continue to make multiracial matches and push for that solution in that area.

We also need to provide more training and support to our mentors in this initiative. For example, suppose I match a mentor, a white male who works at CocaCola, with a black boy who lives on the westside of Atlanta. In that case, I need to make sure that white male mentor is ready for this experience. So we're going to beef up our training and provide more support and more screening to ensure we're making the right match.

Suppose someone is just starting their mentoring journey. In that case, we are making sure they have the proper resources and have the right reasons as a foundation. We also want to support training on the history of black people in America. The history of systemic racism, the history of racism in Atlanta, and especially the Civil Rights Movement. All of these pieces play a role in ensuring that when we make a biracial match, both sides are ready to be a part of that. These are some of the things that we are working on, and we're just getting started with the depth of the impact we can make.

It's an exciting time now for us to be impactful. With a strong financial footing, cash reserve, endowment, and enough resources to make investments into our programs, we will improve our work. In addition to selling our headquarters in Midtown, we also launched a $2M capacity-building campaign to fund different projects that will enable us to serve more students and families. We completed the campaign in record-breaking time and raised $2M within six months during Covid. Many foundations in Atlanta and our board of directors stepped up to help us raise the money. The money will enable us to beef up our staff and capacity in the areas of fundraising, marketing, and DEI. Lastly, the money will pay for the build-out of our new office and enable us to pilot some new programs and our satellite approach to better serve our Littles and Bigs.

Everything we do is for the kids. Despite the challenges we've faced since Covid, we've powered through to continue to support our community and the kids who need it most. We've defended their potential and watched our work bloom and grow. We work to be a Steve Maynord, Bob Woodson, or Terence Mathis for someone else. We work to support kids like me who need a second chance in life. Every day at Big Brothers Big Sisters, we work to preserve the dreams and potential that lives within each and every kid. We mentor because mentorship is power. It gives the kids we serve the ability to own their stories. It shows them that no matter who they are or where they come from, their story is important, and one day it will be their story that changes the world.

To The Little Brothers and Little Sisters of The World

Never forget that your story is your super-power. Many young people do not live within their story, share their story, and are uncomfortable with it. The reality is, your story will set you apart from the rest of the world. Never forget your upbringing, the trials, and the tribulations you have conquered. Never forget your first love and how you felt at the most critical moments of your life. All of these things are who you are.

Growing up in high school and in college, you hear about becoming a doctor or lawyer, which are all great professions. But, it is not often that you hear about a CEO of a nonprofit organization doing work to help people who are just like him. I want you to know this critical fact: There are careers and journeys on this side of the nonprofit sector where you can do good work to make a difference no matter who you are or what you have been through. It is a requirement for you to drive wherever you end up to a better place somehow. You have to figure out what that means for you and your passion. There is one rule in this life: To make the world a better place.

CONCLUSION: THE MONUMENT

The people, places, and things we don't save will be lost. The people, places, and things we reserve will be found.

|KJ|

There is only one thing that is certain in this life, and it is change. The people, places, and things around you will inevitably change. More importantly, you will undergo tremendous changes in your lifetime.

Change is what fuels The Hope Inside. The need, want, and desire to be better, to dream bigger and stand taller as you work to will the life that is rightfully yours into existence. Greatness is your birthright. Yet the perils of this world, the injustice, inequality, and the at times inhumane messaging that we take in and absorb to be our own will lead us to forget about who and whose we are. The visions of distraught and despair that you encounter at times have the power to appear more prevalent than the abundance that we have access to, and that is rightfully ours. Simply put, we run the risk of making poor decisions when we fail to remember our power.

It took me what felt like a lifetime to find peace with everything that has happened to me, but I found it. If I have not made it clear throughout the pages of this book, allow me to state again that I own everything that has happened to me. The good, the bad, and even the darkest moments of my life. More importantly, I use it as inspiration to fuel my future.

Eventually, I went back to visit Judge Aloi. Contrary to what most would be, I am grateful for his sentence. I stood face to face with him in his chambers, shackled no more, and thanked him. The truth is that prison became a building block of the solid foundation I stand on today. I would not be who I am had I not had that experience. I also thanked him for sealing my record and giving me a second chance. At the time, hearing that I would be required to serve a year felt like an eternity, but it did not destroy me. I didn't think that when it happened to me, but I saw it differently as I got older. My words felt like air, and on that day, he cried.

He said, "Kwame, in all the years I've been a judge, and in the thousands of people I've sentenced before, no one has ever come back for the right reason. Ever."

164

I was there that day for the right reasons. I had learned the lesson I was meant to retain from life for the right reasons. And today, I am a living vessel of service to youth who deserve the glimmer of hope in their eyes for the right reasons.

Quotable by Kwame Johnson, Sr.

"We will never become what we want by remaining what we are."

"You can not change the beginning of your story, the cards you were dealt, or your life's circumstances, but you have unprecedented power to manifest the life you believe you deserve."

"If you're afraid, consider it a victory. No limits are broken in the zone of comfort."

"You don't have to announce your internal changes to the world, bloom where you are planted."

"Get excited about what could go right."

"Commit to your dreams, not your zone of comfort."

167

Stories of Success: Katy

Meet former Little Sister Katy and Big Sister Gretchen

Big Sister Gretchen and Little Sister Katy were **matched for more than six years** before Katy's graduation in May 2018. Over the years, they have developed a very loving and supportive bond that has helped Katy become the young woman she is today.

At the beginning of their match, Katy's mother identified what she considered to be the two most important goals for Gretchen to help Katy work on—developing greater self-confidence and improving her academic performance. Katy has

Big Brothers
Big Sisters.
OF METRO ATLANTA

excelled in both areas, all while experiencing many life struggles. She has earned numerous academic awards and achievements, including the Georgia Certificate of Merit, AP Scholar, Junior Marshall, and Quest bridge finalist. In high school, she served as president of the HOPE (Hispanic Organization Promoting Education) Club, secretary of the Spanish Club, and was active in the National Beta Club and the Science Olympiad Club.

Katy says, "I don't know where I would be without Ms. Gretchen. She truly has been there for me through thick and thin and has shown me so much love and support". Katy's mother also expressed her gratitude for Katy's Big Sister by saying, **"Gretchen came into my daughter's life when Katy needed it most, and I will be forever grateful to her. She has not only been her support system but mine as well being a single mom."**

Gretchen served a vital role in making sure Katy excelled in school; she was quick to provide help when she could. When she couldn't  assist with a particular subject, she made it her duty to find Katy the help she needed. As a result, Katy graduated from high school in May 2018 as an honor graduate with a 3.92 GPA.

Big Sister Gretchen stated, "I truly consider Katy as my little sister, and **it has been such a blessing to have her and her family in my life**." She describes Katy as "a kind, determined, and a golden-hearted person who is just a joy to be with."

At the June 2018 Big Brothers Big Sisters Graduation Celebration, Katy was one of two graduating seniors in our program awarded a scholarship towards her college education. In accepting the award, Katy thanked "**everyone who believed in me even when I didn't believe in myself.**"

Here is what her Big Sister Gretchen had to say in nominating Katy for the award: "Katy is extremely deserving of the scholarship. She is **hardworking, dedicated, and humble and has a strong desire to succeed**. Despite her economic challenges, her humil-

ity, care for others, and willingness to sacrifice her own wants and needs for others is awe-inspiring."

Katy is currently a Sophomore at the University of Southern California, majoring in Computational Neuroscience.

More recently, Katy was honored again at the Big Brothers Big Sisters 2019 Legacy Awards Gala. Katy was chosen as the **recipient of the Big Futures scholarship**, presented by Arthur and Angela Blank. This scholarship enables Katy to continue her post-secondary education and achieve her goals and dreams for the future.

STORIES OF SUCCESS: MIKE

Former Little Brother Mike Auzenne is Director of Marketing Analytics at Inspire Brands. After excelling in high school, Mike graduated from Colgate University, worked in the investment banking industry in New York, and later earned his MBA from Harvard Business School. He credits his Big Brother Austin with helping shape him into the person he is today. We would like to share a bit of Mike and Austin's one on one mentoring relationship:

Mike was matched with his Big Brother Austin when he was nine years old. Mike's mother was a single parent, and she wanted Mike to have a male role model and someone who would help provide structure in his life. Austin modeled hard work and commitment for Mike not only in sports and academics but in all other areas of life.

Their shared experiences helped prepare Mike for an academic and professional path over the years. A path that Mike might not have known existed if not for Austin's involvement in his life.

Mike says, "Your future is often largely dependent on what you're exposed to. There are a lot of kids that do not have the opportunity to reach their full potential due to their circumstances, whether it be a single parent, socioeconomic status, where they live, etc."

When Mike floundered in his first semester of high school, he describes how "Austin stepped in and worked with me to lay out a plan with specific goals to set me up to be accepted to college. Soon, I began surpassing expectations in the classroom, on the basketball court, and on the football field. I worked hard, stayed humble, and carried myself with integrity. He expected me to do great things, and I learned that I was capable of far more than I thought possible. All I needed was someone to hold me accountable. My Big Brother put me on a path where I believed I could succeed, regardless of the obstacles in front of me."

Recognizing his mentor's tremendous impact on his life, Mike wanted to pay it forward. He continues advocating for Big Brothers Big Sisters in many ways. Most importantly, for almost four years, Mike has been Big Brother to his Little Brother Justice, now thirteen years old, whose father is incarcerated. Mike provides Justice with the same friendship, guidance, and support he received from his own Big Brother, helping him discover and develop his full potential.

Kwame's Power Playlist

Music is such a big part of my life. Music has served as the backdrop for some of my most teachable life lessons. It also kept me inspired along the way. I've chosen eleven songs that will inspire you when reading this book.

Happy listening!

1. Jay Z featuring Alicia Keys, "Empire State of Mind"
2. 112, "Cupid"
3. Santana, "Oye Como Va"
4. Drake, "Started From the Bottom"
5. Isaac Hayes, "The Look Of Love" (Dead Presidents Soundtrack)
6. Elton John, "I'm Still Standing"
7. Keyshia Cole, "Take Me Away"
8. Capone-N-Noreaga featuring Carl Thomas, "I Love My Life"
9. Survivor, "Eye of the Tiger"
10. Mary J. Blige, "I Love You"
11. Mogwai, "Auto Rock" (Miami Vice Soundtrack)